MW00962749

# Cyber Bullying

# Cyber Bullying

## A Prevention Curriculum for Grades 6–12

Susan P. Limber, Ph.D.

Robin M. Kowalski, Ph.D.

Patricia W. Agatston, Ph.D.

HAZELDEN®

Hazelden
Center City, MN 55012
hazelden.org

© 2008, 2014 by Hazelden Foundation, all language versions worldwide
All rights reserved. First edition published 2008.
Updated and revised edition published 2014.
Printed in the United States of America

No part of this publication may be reproduced, stored in a retrieval system, or
transmitted in any form or by any means—electronic, mechanical, photocopying,
recording, scanning, or otherwise—without the express written permission of
the publisher, except for the reproducible handouts and templates, as indicated.
Failure to comply with these terms may expose you to legal action and damages
for copyright infringement.

ISBN: 978-1-61649-583-1

The names, details, and circumstances may have been changed to protect the privacy of
those mentioned in this publication.

Design and production by David Farr, ImageSmythe, and Terri Kinne
Interior illustrations by Chris Dyrud
Cover design by David Spohn

# Endorsements

"Schools and other youth-serving professionals are often looking for turnkey programming they can easily and immediately implement to deal with the problem of cyberbullying. This age-appropriate curriculum is chock-full of informed, user-friendly, and interactive scenario-based learning opportunities and activities for teens. It makes it simple for teachers and other supervisory adults to take it and run with it—and help make a positive difference in the attitudes and behaviors of the student body."

—Sameer Hinduja, codirector of the Cyberbullying Research Center
and professor of Criminology at Florida Atlantic University

"Older students use the news events from the curriculum and have small group discussions, comparing the events to what they experience in real life or hear about in our news. Most important, students learn how to treat their peers with respect and kindness and develop the skills to respond positively when they are confronted with negative behavior online and offline, or get help when necessary."

—Anna Arnold, Family Resource and Safe Schools coordinator
for Henry County Schools, Henry County, Georgia

Duplicating this page is illegal. Do not copy this material without written permission from the publisher.

# Contents

Duplicating this page is illegal. Do not copy this material without written permission from the publisher.

# Acknowledgments

We would like to thank Alyse Cooper-Pribish of the Lovett School, Stephanie Meyer of Kennesaw Mountain High School, Jennie Brown and Jason Christy of Cayuse Prairie School, and Harriet Zimmer of the Balmoral Hill School, who along with their students provided invaluable feedback and suggestions for our curriculum. We also are indebted to Marlene Snyder, Ph.D., for her extremely helpful comments on an earlier draft. Bonnie Dudovitz and the editorial team of Jenny Miller and Sue Thomas at Hazelden Publishing helped shepherd the development of this curriculum. Without their support, creativity, and assistance, this project would not have been produced. Finally, we thank our families—Andrew, Austin, Jack, Noah, Jordan, and Mary—who continue to inspire and support our work.

A special thanks from the publisher goes to Angie Laehn, eighth-grade English teacher at Pepin Middle School, Pepin, Wisconsin, and students Tanner Luhmann and Kassandra Heit for their help in reviewing this text for the latest technological terms.

Duplicating this page is illegal. Do not copy this material without written permission from the publisher.

ix

# How to Access the Resources on the CD-ROM

The accompanying CD-ROM contains print resources, including electronic versions of the curriculum's handouts and templates and related research information. All of these resources are in PDF format and can be accessed using Adobe Reader.® If you do not have Adobe Reader, you can download it for free at www.adobe.com.

The icon ⬚ in this guide means the needed resource is located on the CD-ROM. The notation that follows this icon indicates the document number for that resource's file. The first letter or letter/number pair indicates which folder the file is located in on the CD-ROM. The CD-ROM file numbers will help you easily locate and print the resource you are looking for. This symbol (SP) indicates the document is also available in Spanish.

To access these print resources, put the disk in your computer's CD-ROM player. Open your version of Adobe Reader. Then open the documents by finding them on your CD-ROM drive. These resources cannot be modified, but they may be printed for use without concern for copyright infringement. For a list of what is contained on the CD-ROM, see the Read Me First document on the CD-ROM.

Duplicating this page is illegal. Do not copy this material without written permission from the publisher.

xi

# Introductory Materials

## Introduction to the Curriculum

### What Is *Cyberbullying: A Prevention Curriculum for Grades 6–12*?

*Cyberbullying: A Prevention Curriculum for Grades 6–12* is a program that deals with attitudes and behaviors associated with cyberbullying. It consists of an eight-session curriculum, with these additional resources:

- reproducible parent* resources

- program posters and student handouts

- resources to address cyberbullying schoolwide (establishing a school policy, addressing legal concerns, etc.)

- peer leader training materials

- a short training on cyberbullying for program facilitators

- a pre-test/post-test that can be conducted before and after implementation of the curriculum to measure student retention

Most materials needed to implement the program are included in this manual and the CD-ROM. In addition, a website has been established that provides up-to-date information about bullying and cyberbullying. This website can be accessed at www.violencepreventionworks.org.

### What Are the Program's Goals?

This program strives to achieve these goals:

- raise students' and parents' awareness of what cyberbullying is and why it is so harmful

* All references to parents in this text also include guardians.

Duplicating this page is illegal. Do not copy this material without written permission from the publisher.

1

- equip students with the skills and resources to treat each other respectfully when using cyber technologies

- give students information about how to get help if they or others they know are being cyberbullied

- teach students how to use cyber technologies in positive ways

- help students become better digital citizens

For more information on the learner outcomes for each session, turn to the Curriculum Scope and Sequence, page 19.

## What Are the Components of *Cyberbullying: A Prevention Curriculum for Grades 6–12?*

### *Eight-Session Curriculum*

Each session can be completed in 50 minutes. The curriculum can be presented over a period of days or weeks, depending on your program's schedule. Each session includes detailed instructions on presenting the information, activities to reinforce the key concepts, and reproducible student handouts.

If you don't have time to present all eight sessions, consider condensing the curriculum into five sessions by omitting session 1 and combining sessions 6–8, with much of the project work in these sessions being completed as homework assignments.

Throughout the curriculum, some activities will be designated for middle school students or high school students. These include small-group discussion situations and a few other activities. These will be marked with the following icons: **Grade 6–8** **Grade 9–12**

 The first five sessions of *Cyberbullying* for students in middle school include journal entries from four fictional students who are learning about cyberbullying. Students will read the journal entries and discuss them in peer-led small groups. These journal entries engage students in the topic of the session and help them understand how to react to cyberbullying situations. The use of these fictional peers has been shown to be an effective teaching tool in evidence-

Duplicating this page is illegal. Do not copy this material without written permission from the publisher.

based programs, such as Hazelden's Project Northland alcohol-use prevention curricula. It is important that you read through all the journal entries before beginning the program in your classroom so that you are aware of the story line and the characters' personalities.

 The first five sessions of *Cyberbullying* for students in high school include real-life stories—one per session. These real-life stories are based on actual events found in the news; however, names and some minor details have been changed and the characters' points of view dramatized. These real-life stories will make cyberbullying real to students and include questions to help spark discussion.

  An idea for presenting both the journal entries and the real-life stories would be to post these online in a blog or chat room. If you do this, be sure to make posting accessible to only you and your students. Should you choose to post this content online, additional homework questions have been included at the end of each session to allow the students to answer online and to encourage them to apply the situations to their own lives.

In sessions 6–7, students will work on a small-group project to create plans for their own social-networking sites or apps. (Students will not actually design sites or apps, just create plans for them.) They will need to meet specific criteria to ensure the websites or apps are safe for the users and promote positive inter-actions among teens. Each small group will present its website or app plan to the class during session 8. You may wish to assign some of this project work as homework or devote more class time to the assignment.

This program also includes a Cyberbullying Pre-Test/Post-Test on pages 31–36 that can be used to assess your students' knowledge and attitudes before and after you present the curriculum.

The curriculum uses peer leaders to lead a significant portion of each lesson, with the last three sessions serving as a cooperative-learning and project-based opportunity. Information about selecting and training peer leaders is found in  I-10 the Peer Leader Packet on the CD-ROM. Peer leadership is a key component of this program and should not be omitted.

It is highly recommended that educators implement this program as part of an ongoing, comprehensive bullying prevention effort, such as the *Olweus Bullying*  I-9 *Prevention Program (OBPP)*. (Olweus is pronounced Ol-vay-us.) More information on linking this curriculum to *OBPP* is provided on the CD-ROM.

Duplicating this page is illegal. Do not copy this material without written permission from the publisher.

The Curriculum Scope and Sequence for the eight sessions is provided on page 19.

I-11 You will find a Glossary of Cyber Terms for your reference on the CD-ROM. You may also wish to send this home for students' parents.

### Parent Materials

I-12 (SP)

I-11

As in every strong prevention effort, it's important to actively involve your students' parents when implementing this program. A letter that informs parents about *Cyberbullying: A Prevention Curriculum for Grades 6–12* is on the CD-ROM. It is recommended that this letter be sent to parents with the Glossary of Cyber Terms, also found on the CD-ROM, prior to implementing the program.

Each of the first five sessions also has a take-home assignment that students should do with a parent. After completing the assignment, adults and students are to sign the assignment and return it. If students are not able to have active parent participation, they can complete the activity with another close adult, such as a relative or neighbor, or if possible, a school staff person, such as a school counselor, may take part in this role.

All parent materials are provided in both English and Spanish.

### Teacher Training Outline

You are encouraged to provide training for others at your school on how to use this curriculum. An outline for a 3-hour teacher training session is provided on pages 131–140. Consider hosting a training session for your school's faculty and staff.

### Teacher Training Presentation

I-14 Included on the CD-ROM is a training presentation that includes in-depth information and statistics on cyberbullying for teachers. This presentation can be used either as a self-led training or as part of the Teacher Training Outline. Instructions on how to use this training are included on the CD-ROM.

Duplicating this page is illegal. Do not copy this material without written permission from the publisher.

## Who Is the Intended Audience?

*Cyberbullying: A Prevention Curriculum for Grades 6–12* is designed for middle and high school students. This program would fit well within a health education, communications, technology, or general life skills curriculum (see Related National Academic Standards, pages 21–24). Information on the Common Core Standards is available at www.violencepreventionworks.org. Teachers may use their discretion to adapt some activities to the ages and maturity levels of their students.

This curriculum involves trained student peer leaders who assist in teaching portions of the sessions. These leaders should be selected by their peers, two weeks prior to starting this curriculum. Encourage students to select fellow students whom they admire and respect. You will find more guidance on the peer leader selection process in the Peer Leader Packet on the CD-ROM. You may also want to consider having older teens teach the program to younger teens.

 I-10

In addition, a school counselor could offer *Cyberbullying* as part of a special educational program, or it could be used in after-school, community, youth-enrichment (such as YMCA or Scouts), or faith-based youth programs.

## Is This a Research-Based Program?

*Cyberbullying* is not a research-based program, but it is based on the latest research in prevention and the topic of cyberbullying. Many of the session activities are patterned after prevention models that research has shown to be effective in decreasing negative student behaviors and increasing student attitudes toward refraining from negative behaviors.

These strategies include selecting and using peer leaders, providing parent-student activities, doing cooperative learning and project activities, and identifying the causes for the reasons students behave as they do.

The curriculum also recommends that schoolwide policies and procedures be established that can effectively address the issue of cyberbullying in a broad way, while establishing a climate conducive to positive interactions among students. Research-based programs, such as the *Olweus Bullying Prevention Program*, have proven that schoolwide efforts are more effective in addressing bullying than classroom components alone.

Duplicating this page is illegal. Do not copy this material without written permission from the publisher.

## How Can We Address Cyberbullying on a Schoolwide Level?

The *Cyberbullying* curriculum should be taught within a school or organizational environment that supports the prevention of all forms of bullying, including cyberbullying.

Here are some ways schools and community organizations can promote and support the message that cyberbullying is not acceptable:

1. Work to create a school environment in which respect and responsibility are promoted and bullying is not.

 I-9

2. In conjunction with this classroom curriculum, implement a schoolwide program, such as the *Olweus Bullying Prevention Program,* to address bullying of all kinds.

 I-1 through I-7

3. Set clear school policies about reporting and addressing cyberbullying, whether or not it occurs on campus. (See the CD-ROM for information about creating school policies.)

4. Train staff to be aware of cyberbullying and to intervene appropriately. A training outline is provided on pages 131–140, and a training presentation is located on the CD-ROM. Have as many staff members as possible complete this training.

I-14

5. If a student or parent reports an incident of cyberbullying, take the situation seriously and proactively address the issue, even if the cyberbullying messages did not originate at your school.

6. Teach the *Cyberbullying* curriculum to all students. Make program participation mandatory. In some cases, you might want to focus on one grade at a time, but make sure all receive it.

7. Host a cyberbullying prevention campaign. Involve students in making posters, announcements, and other promotional materials on this important issue. You may also want to use the posters included on the CD-ROM.

 I-15

8. Make young people aware of the resources in your school and in your community that are available to help them if they experience cyberbullying. Have a panel where older students (high school) serving as peer leaders discuss digital citizenship with younger students.

Duplicating this page is illegal. Do not copy this material without written permission from the publisher.

9. Involve parents by hosting education programs for them and sending home the introductory parent letter and the parent-student homework assignments provided with each lesson in this curriculum.

10. Establish procedures that parents can follow in reporting cyberbullying incidents to school staff. Make sure parents and staff know what these procedures are, and be sure to proactively address any cyberbullying incidents.

## What Resources Are Available Online or in My Community to Help with This Topic?

You don't need to be an expert on cyberbullying to teach this curriculum. However, you may want to turn to community resources for help in presenting this issue or to learn more about it.

Most local law-enforcement agencies can provide guidance on how to address crimes related to cyberbullying. They may also be able to give guidance on how to track the source of anonymous cyberbullying messages.

The websites Connect Safely and Common Sense Media provide information and resources on the digital technologies and social media sites that are popular with youth.

Pages 141–143 of this curriculum list additional resources available to you and to parents as you teach this curriculum.

## What Should I Be Aware of When Teaching *Cyberbullying: A Prevention Curriculum for Grades 6–12?*

Here are some helpful tips for teaching this curriculum:

1. During the first session, it's important to create a sense of trust and safety in your group. Be sure to discuss the need for ground rules (as outlined below). Make sure students abide by these rules throughout the program.

2. When in a group setting, make sure students do not use real names or too many details when describing cyberbullying situations that they or

Duplicating this page is illegal. Do not copy this material without written permission from the publisher.

7

others have experienced. Encourage them to share any specific concerns they may have with you in private.

3. Be aware that some students in your class may be experiencing bullying, or cyberbullying in particular. Don't force students to answer questions or talk about their experiences if they're uncomfortable doing so.

4. Be aware that some students in your class may be bullying others.

5. It's difficult in a class environment to guarantee complete confidentiality. Warn students of this fact, so they don't reveal more than they are comfortable with. Also warn students ahead of time that if they reveal information about someone being hurt by others or someone who is considering hurting himself or herself, you are required to report this information.

6. Maintain respect during discussions. Allow people to offer opposing views, but to do so respectfully.

7. Peer leaders are a key component of this curriculum. As much as possible, allow students to select the peer leaders. If they choose someone who is known to be bullying others or is a negative peer leader, you may want to override their selection. On the other hand, the experience of leading others in bullying prevention efforts may have a strong influence on that student's behavior in the future. Supervision of all peer leaders is recommended to ensure they are not abusing their roles.

### What Are Some Other Guidelines to Follow as I Teach *Cyberbullying: A Prevention Curriculum for Grades 6–12*?

1. *What if a student reveals she or he or a friend is being cyberbullied or bullied in other ways?*

   Before teaching this curriculum, check whether your school has a policy on reporting cyberbullying or bullying of any kind. If you are uncertain about reporting procedures, talk with your school leadership about how incidents should be reported.

Duplicating this page is illegal. Do not copy this material without written permission from the publisher.

While you are teaching this curriculum, a student may reveal that he or she is either being cyberbullied or is cyberbullying others. As previously noted, it's important at the outset of the program to let students know what you will do upon learning this information, so they don't feel set up or betrayed by the action you take.

If a student reveals information during a class discussion, do not continue discussing the issue with everyone present. Invite the student to talk privately with you afterward. Write down any information the student provides.

Don't try to solve this problem on your own. Consult with appropriate school officials and the student's parents.

2. *What should I do if, while visiting a social-networking site, I find examples of cyberbullying among my students?*

As you become more familiar with digital technologies that students are using, you may find instances in which students in your school or district are engaged in cyberbullying or other worrisome behaviors on the Internet. Whenever possible, print out the information and share it with your school leadership. In most cases, inappropriate information added to social-networking sites can be traced back to the person who created it. Often just notifying the parents of the parties involved may be enough to resolve the issues. However, depending on the seriousness of the issue, you may need to involve law-enforcement officials.

3. *What if parents are uncomfortable with the topic and don't want their children involved?*

On rare occasions, parents may express reservations about their child or children being taught this cyberbullying prevention curriculum. This may occur because some parents may not want their child or children using certain digital technologies or may be concerned about Internet safety.

While participating in the cyberbullying prevention program, students will not be working online except where optionally suggested. Care has also been taken to make sure the program does not give students new ideas of how to cyberbully one another.

Duplicating this page is illegal. Do not copy this material without written permission from the publisher.

When parents raise concerns, encourage them to review the curriculum.
Tell them about the prevalence of cyberbullying among teens and the
importance of addressing this issue in a preventative way. Discuss any
additional concerns they may have. If they still voice reservations, it may
be best to have the students complete an alternate project on a related
topic.

I-12 (SP)

Be sure to let parents know about the curriculum in advance through
school newsletters or informational meetings and by sending home a
letter explaining the curriculum. You will find a sample letter on the
CD-ROM.

Duplicating this page is illegal. Do not copy this material without written permission from the publisher.

# Introduction to Cyberbullying

Danielle was a new student at the middle school. It was hard making new friends and finding ways to fit in. For some reason, the popular girls in her class didn't like her. They called her names and told her not to sit anywhere near them in the cafeteria.

The bullying became even worse when these girls decided to create a page on a popular social-networking site where they posted unflattering pictures of Danielle and wrote terrible messages.

Danielle found out about it when she saw several girls secretly looking at a computer and laughing in the library. Danielle was shocked to see the website, but she didn't want to tell any adults because she feared the cyberbullying might get even worse.

For many students like Danielle, cyberbullying is a serious issue that affects their sense of well-being and their ability to learn in the classroom. To understand what cyberbullying is, it is important to first understand what bullying is.

## What Is Bullying?

Dan Olweus, Ph.D., a pioneer researcher in the area of bullying, has defined bullying in this way:

> Bullying is when someone repeatedly and on purpose says or does mean or hurtful things to another person who has a hard time defending himself or herself (Olweus et al. 2007, xii).

Duplicating this page is illegal. Do not copy this material without written permission from the publisher.

There are both direct and indirect forms of bullying. More direct forms include physical actions such as hitting someone, taking or damaging someone else's things, or saying mean or hurtful things to someone.

Indirect forms of bullying are more concealed and subtle, and it is more difficult to determine who is causing the bullying. Examples include social exclusion, spreading rumors, and cyberbullying.

Dr. Olweus's research determined that students play a variety of roles in bullying situations. These roles make up what he termed the "Bullying Circle." These roles are diagrammed below (Snyder et al. 2014, 17–18).

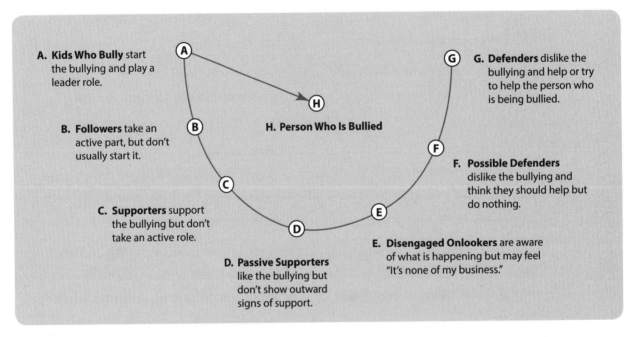

The Bullying Circle and roles are taken from Snyder, Marlene, Jane Riese, Susan P. Limber, Dan Olweus, and Stein Gorseth. 2014. *Olweus Bullying Prevention Program: Community Youth Organization Guide.* Center City, MN: Hazelden Publishing.

Here is a description of each role:

A. **Kids Who Bully** others start the bullying and play a leader role. For example, they select the person to be bullied and how to harm him or her.

B. **Followers** want to be liked by those who bully. They take an active part in the bullying, or bully others as they're told to do, but don't usually start it.

C. **Supporters** support the bullying, maybe by laughing or encouraging, but they don't take an active role.

Duplicating this page is illegal. Do not copy this material without written permission from the publisher.

**D. Passive Supporters** like the bullying but don't show outward signs of support.

**E. Disengaged Onlookers** are aware of what is happening but may feel "It's none of my business."

**F. Possible Defenders** dislike the bullying and think they should help the person who is being bullied, but they do nothing.

**G. Defenders** dislike the bullying and help or try to help the **Person Who Is Bullied.**

**H.** This is the **Person Who Is Bullied.**

In effective bullying prevention efforts, it is helpful to focus on changing the attitudes and behaviors of bystanders, who generally make up 80 percent of a school's student body. The goal is to move these bystanders into the position of defending or helping the student who is being bullied. This is a primary goal of *Cyberbullying: A Prevention Curriculum for Grades 6–12.*

## What Is Cyberbullying?

Cyberbullying is bullying through email or instant messaging, in a chat room, on a website or an online gaming site, or through digital messages or video images sent to a cell phone (Kowalski, Limber, and Agatston 2012). Cyberbullying, like traditional bullying, involves a negative action that is often repeated and includes an imbalance of power.

In traditional forms of bullying, individuals may have more power over another by being bigger, stronger, or more popular. With cyberbullying, an individual may have more power just by being able to instantly share negative comments or photographs with a multitude of people via email, instant messaging, text messaging, or through social-networking site posts. Cyberbullying may also involve several individuals targeting one individual or a more popular student targeting a less popular classmate.

Traditional bullying is also defined by mean or negative actions being repeated and occurring over time. When someone is cyberbullied, this repetition of negative behavior can occur by sending one embarrassing photo or one degrading email

Duplicating this page is illegal. Do not copy this material without written permission from the publisher.

message, which may in turn be forwarded to an entire class or grade level. The person doing traditional bullying is usually known, but he or she might go unidentified in the case of cyberbullying.

Traditional bullying usually occurs in a certain time and space, perhaps during school in the bathrooms or the hallways. Students who are bullied can usually find some relief at home or away from school. When a student is cyberbullied, the incident can happen whenever someone turns on his or her computer or accesses the Internet. This often happens at home at any time of the day or night.

Cyberbullying poses unique challenges because it frequently happens outside the school setting, and thus may be difficult for educators to observe. In addition, students may feel invisible or anonymous while online, which may lead to a greater willingness to engage in negative actions. Finally, without face-to-face interaction, students who cyberbully have no opportunity to witness the emotional distress their comments may be inflicting on a peer.

There is a bright spot, however. While direct evidence may be hard to obtain in many traditional forms of bullying, cyberbullying typically involves a form of communication that can be saved and printed from a computer or saved on a cell phone. Such obvious evidence can be helpful when intervening in cyberbullying incidences.

## Why Should Schools Address the Issue of Cyberbullying?

Schools have rapidly embraced technology because of its ability to offer advanced learning opportunities and resources to students. Teachers use blogs, students post assignments online, and some schools issue laptops or tablets to students as instructional tools. By embracing technology and encouraging students to explore its various forms, educators also have a duty to teach students to use such technologies in a responsible manner.

In addition, many schools are already adopting comprehensive bullying prevention programs, such as the *Olweus Bullying Prevention Program,* or are at least teaching classroom lessons that address bullying behaviors. Cyberbullying is one form of bullying that should be specifically addressed as part of these comprehensive efforts.

Duplicating this page is illegal. Do not copy this material without written permission from the publisher.

Research has shown that not all students perceive cyberbullying as a form of bullying behavior (Kowalski, Limber, and Agatston 2012). Therefore, classroom lessons and discussions that focus directly on cyberbullying are critical to preventing it from flourishing.

## What Is the Prevalence of Cyberbullying?

While the numbers vary based on the methods used to gather the data, the National Crime Victimization Survey found that 9 percent of students in grades 6–12 had been cyberbullied during the 2011 school year (Robers et al. 2013). In addition, Kowalski and Limber (2007) found that 18 percent of middle school students had been cyberbullied and 11 percent had cyberbullied others at least once in the previous couple of months. Thus, high percentages of students are being affected by this behavior.

## What Are the Warning Signs of Cyberbullying?

The warning signs of cyberbullying are similar to those for traditional bullying in terms of emotional effects; however, there are some differences. For example, we would not expect to see bruises or torn clothing on a child who is being cyberbullied. However, it is also important to keep in mind that some students who are cyberbullied may also be experiencing traditional bullying at school.

A child may be experiencing cyberbullying if he or she

- appears sad, moody, or anxious.

- avoids school.

- withdraws from or shows a lack of interest in social activities.

- experiences a drop in grades or decline in academic performance.

- appears upset after using the computer or being online.

- appears upset after viewing a text message.

If a student shows any of these warning signs, it is important to talk with the student and investigate the student's online presence to determine if cyberbullying is occurring and to offer help where needed.

Duplicating this page is illegal. Do not copy this material without written permission from the publisher.

## How Is Cyberbullying Affecting Students, Schools, and Communities?

Current research demonstrates that students who are targets of traditional bullying are more likely to have low self-esteem (Olweus 1993; Rigby and Slee 1993), be anxious and depressed (Prancjić and Bajraktarević 2010; Wang, Nansel, and Ianotti 2011), and experience a variety of health problems such as stomachaches, headaches, fatigue, and difficulty sleeping and eating (Fekkes, Pijpers, and Verloove-VanHorick 2004) than students not involved with traditional bullying. They also are more likely to exhibit suicidal thoughts and behaviors (Espelage and Holt 2013; Klomek et al. 2008). Students who are being targeted by peer abuse, such as cyberbullying, are not likely to give their full attention to academics and may even be afraid to come to school. Students who are bullied have higher absenteeism rates and lower grades than students who are not bullied (Arseneault et al. 2006; Eisenberg, Neumark-Sztainer, and Perry 2003; Nakamoto and Schwartz 2010).

Research on cyberbullying specifically suggests that students involved in cyberbullying (particularly those who are cyberbullied and who also cyberbully others) are more likely to be anxious, to be depressed, and to have low self-esteem than students who are not involved (Kowalski et al. 2014; Kowalski and Limber 2013). Students who are cyberbullied are also more likely to have lower grades and higher absenteeism rates than those students not involved (Kowalski et al. 2014; Kowalski and Limber 2013).

Although cyberbullying usually occurs outside of the school day, it can impact school when students are afraid to face their peer group after receiving mean comments or messages at home. In addition, many students are targets of traditional bullying at school and cyberbullying at home, which can leave them feeling that no safe haven is available to them.

Educators and administrators frequently observe that investigating and intervening in cyberbullying incidents can be very time-consuming. Parents also report feeling victimized when their children are targeted by cyberbullying (Kowalski, Limber, and Agatston 2012). Just as schools discuss character education for the real world, they need to discuss how students treat one another in the online world as technology advances.

Duplicating this page is illegal. Do not copy this material without written permission from the publisher.

## What Should Teachers Do If They Know or Suspect Cyberbullying Is Occurring?

It is important to educate students about how to report all forms of bullying, including cyberbullying, to adults at school and at home. This should be part of a teacher's ongoing classroom discussions about bullying. Session 5 in this curriculum also teaches students these skills.

If a teacher suspects a student is being cyberbullied, he or she should advise the student to save any evidence of the cyberbullying and report it by attaching a copy of the printed online communications as evidence. The teacher can also recommend or share information or links on reporting abuse to social-networking sites. The student can bring the evidence to the teacher, a school counselor, or an administrator. If there is no evidence, the student should still report the cyberbullying and include a description of what is taking place, so that a counselor or administrator can investigate and speak with the parties involved.

Although all adults at school should have an understanding of cyberbullying and should be open to receiving reports of cyberbullying, it will be most helpful if there are identified individuals at each school who are particularly knowledgeable about bullying and cyberbullying. These individuals will want to investigate and determine if there is any on-campus traditional bullying and/or cyberbullying accompanying off-campus cyberbullying.

Any evidence of bullying at school should be addressed with consistent consequences for the student engaged in bullying behavior and with heightened adult supervision around the targeted student. In addition, positive bystanders should be encouraged to support the targeted student through a variety of means, such as those suggested in this curriculum. Check with your school administrators to determine the appropriate person to whom cyberbullying incidences should be reported.

Some forms of cyberbullying are illegal. Educators should always contact law enforcement if communications involve death threats, extortion, intimidation, or harassment based on race, religion, gender, or sexual orientation, and any evidence of sexual exploitation (Kowalski, Limber, and Agatston 2012; Willard 2007). See the CD-ROM for additional guidance about legal issues and cyberbullying.

I-1 through I-3

Duplicating this page is illegal. Do not copy this material without written permission from the publisher.

17

If the cyberbullying takes place off campus, does not potentially violate the law, and is not accompanied by on-campus bullying, educators may be somewhat more limited in the actions they can take (e.g., sanctions may violate a student's First Amendment rights). But they can still take steps to intervene by conferencing separately with the students involved and their parents. Teachers can try to monitor any interactions between the involved students more closely, or perhaps they can change class schedules to minimize the contact between the students. They can advise the student who is bullied to save the evidence in case the situation escalates. School counselors might also get involved by arranging a meeting between the students to resolve the situation, although care must be taken in doing so (for a discussion of these sensitive situations, see Kowalski, Limber, and Agatston 2012). Educators can also assist the parents of a targeted student by providing educational literature on preventing and responding to cyberbullying, as well as giving them information on how to report offensive profiles to social-networking sites. This educational literature is provided on the CD-ROM.

I-5

I-6
through
I-8

I-13

Duplicating this page is illegal. Do not copy this material without written permission from the publisher.

# Curriculum Scope and Sequence

| Session 1: What Is Bullying? | Session 2: What Is Cyberbullying? | Session 3: How Does Cyberbullying Affect People? | Session 4: Why Do People Cyberbully Others? |
|---|---|---|---|
| *By the end of this session, students will be able to do the following:* | | | |
| • define *bullying* <br> • identify examples of bullying <br> • identify the roles students play in the Bullying Circle <br> • identify rules against bullying | • define *cyberbullying* <br> • identify the technologies used in cyberbullying <br> • identify cyberbullying situations | • identify the effects of cyberbullying on the student who is bullied, on bystanders, and on the students who bully <br> • identify how to use technology in a positive way | • identify reasons people think they can cyberbully others <br> • state why they think cyberbullying is unacceptable |

| Session 5: How Should You React to Cyberbullying? | Session 6: Creating a Positive Social-Networking Site or App, Part I | Session 7: Creating a Positive Social-Networking Site or App, Part II | Session 8: Creating a Positive Social-Networking Site or App, Part III |
|---|---|---|---|
| *By the end of this session, students will be able to do the following:* | | | |
| • identify what steps to take if they are cyberbullied <br> • identify what steps to take if they know someone else is being cyberbullied | • describe how some social-networking sites began <br> • explain what social-networking sites do to curb abuse <br> • describe the steps in planning a social-networking site or app <br> • describe rules for belonging to some social-networking sites | • describe the components of an effective presentation <br> • identify how they personally will commit themselves to stop or prevent cyberbullying | • make a public commitment to prevent cyberbullying <br> • identify positive ways to use social-networking sites |

For information on how *Cyberbullying: A Prevention Curriculum for Grades 6–12* can help you meet Common Core Standards, see www.violencepreventionworks.org.

Duplicating this page is illegal. Do not copy this material without written permission from the publisher.

Using *Cyberbullying: A Prevention Curriculum for Grades 6–12* will help you meet the following national academic standards. In addition, using *Cyberbullying* will help you meet several Common Core Standards; see www.violencepreventionworks.org for more information.

### Health Education Standards*

***Standard 2:*** Analyze the influence of family, peers, culture, media, technology, and other factors on health behaviors.

Students in grades 6–8 will

- describe how peers influence healthy and unhealthy behaviors.

- analyze how the school and community can affect personal health practices and behaviors.

- analyze how messages from media influence health behaviors.

- analyze the influence of technology on personal and family health.

***Standard 4:*** Demonstrate the ability to use interpersonal communication skills to enhance health and avoid or reduce health risks.

Students in grades 6–8 will

- apply effective verbal and nonverbal communication skills to enhance health.

- demonstrate how to ask for assistance to enhance the health of self and others.

---

\* Joint Committee on National Health Education Standards. 2007. *National Health Education Standards: Achieving Excellence.* 2nd ed. Atlanta, GA: American Cancer Society.

Duplicating this page is illegal. Do not copy this material without written permission from the publisher.

*Standard 7:* Demonstrate the ability to practice health-enhancing behaviors and avoid or reduce health risks.

Students in grades 6–8 will

- demonstrate behaviors that avoid or reduce health risks to self and others.

*Standard 8:* Demonstrate the ability to advocate for personal, family, and community health.

Students in grades 6–8 will

- work cooperatively to advocate for healthy individuals, families, and schools.

- identify ways in which health messages and communication techniques can be altered for different audiences.

*Standard 2:* Analyze the influence of family, peers, culture, media, technology, and other factors on health behaviors.

Students in grades 9–12 will

- analyze how peers influence healthy and unhealthy behaviors.

- evaluate how the school and community can affect personal health practice and behaviors.

- evaluate the effect of media on personal and family health.

- evaluate the impact of technology on personal, family, and community health.

*Standard 4:* Demonstrate the ability to use interpersonal communication skills to enhance health and avoid or reduce health risks.

Students in grades 9–12 will

- use skills for communicating effectively with family, peers, and others to enhance health.

- demonstrate how to ask for and offer assistance to enhance the health of self and others.

*Standard 7:* Demonstrate the ability to practice health-enhancing behaviors and avoid or reduce health risks.

Students in grades 9–12 will

Duplicating this page is illegal. Do not copy this material without written permission from the publisher.

- demonstrate a variety of behaviors that avoid or reduce health risks to self and others.

***Standard 8:*** Demonstrate the ability to advocate for personal, family, and community health.

Students in grades 9–12 will

- work cooperatively as an advocate for improving personal, family, and community health.

- adapt health messages and communication techniques to a specific target audience.

## Technology Education Standards*

### *Communication and Collaboration*

Students in grades 6–12 will

- interact, collaborate, and publish with peers, experts, or others, employing a variety of digital environments and media.

- communicate information and ideas effectively to multiple audiences using a variety of media and formats.

- contribute to project teams to produce original works or solve problems.

### *Critical Thinking, Problem-Solving, and Decision-Making*

Students in grades 6–12 will

- identify and define authentic problems and significant questions for investigation.

- plan and manage activities to develop a solution or complete a project.

- collect and analyze data to identify solutions and make informed decisions.

- use multiple processes and diverse perspectives to explore alternate solutions.

---

\* Reprinted with permission from *National Educational Technology Standards For Teachers* and *National Educational Technology Standards For Students.* Copyright © 2007, 2008 by ISTE (International Society for Technology in Education). All rights reserved.

Duplicating this page is illegal. Do not copy this material without written permission from the publisher.

## Digital Citizenship

Students in grades 6–12 will

- advocate and practice safe, legal, and responsible use of information and technology.

- exhibit a positive attitude toward using technology that supports collaboration, learning, and productivity.

- demonstrate personal responsibility for lifelong learning.

- exhibit leadership for digital citizenship.

Duplicating this page is illegal. Do not copy this material without written permission from the publisher.

## Session Description and Preparation

Here is an overview of the preparation you'll need to do to teach each *Cyberbullying* session.

| Session Title | Session Description | Materials Needed | Preparation Needed |
|---|---|---|---|
| **Session 1: What Is Bullying?** | Through student journal entries or a real-life story, small- and large-group discussions, and word collages, students will define *bullying* and learn about the Bullying Circle diagram and the rules against bullying. | • CD-ROM materials<br>• Parent Letter 📄 I-12 (SP)<br>• Completed Why Should We Talk About Cyberbullying? peer leader handouts 📄 I-10<br>• **Grade 6-8** Session 1 Journal Entries 📄 S1-1<br>• **Grade 9-12** Session 1 Real-Life Story 📄 S1-2<br>• The Bullying Circle diagram 📄 S1-3<br>• The Four Anti-Bullying Rules poster 📄 S1-4<br>• Homework Assignment 1 📄 S1-5 (SP)<br>• *Optional:* Smart Board or whiteboard<br>• Collage materials | • Print out and send the Parent Letter home with each student prior to starting the program.<br>• **Grade 6-8** Copy the Session 1 Journal Entries.<br>• **Grade 9-12** Copy the Session 1 Real-Life Story.<br>• Gather the collage materials.<br>• Copy Homework Assignment 1.<br>• Read through all the journal entries for sessions 1–6.<br>• Return the Why Should We Talk About Cyberbullying? handouts to their peer leader authors.<br>• *Optional:* Write the Bullying Circle diagram and the Four Anti-Bullying Rules onto a whiteboard. If using a Smart Board, have the CD-ROM documents ready to show. |

Duplicating this page is illegal. Do not copy this material without written permission from the publisher.

| Session Title | Session Description | Materials Needed | Preparation Needed |
|---|---|---|---|
| **Session 2: What Is Cyberbullying?** | Through student journal entries or a real-life story, small- and large-group discussions, and a board game, students will understand what cyberbullying is and is not, and the technologies used to cyberbully. | • CD-ROM materials<br>  • **Grade 6–8** Session 2 Journal Entries 🖥 **S2-1**<br>  • **Grade 9–12** Session 2 Real-Life Story 🖥 **S2-2**<br>  • Is It or Isn't It? game board 🖥 **S2-4**<br>  • Is It or Isn't It? game cards 🖥 **S2-5**<br>  • Is It or Isn't It? Peer Leader Instructions 🖥 **S2-3**<br>  • Homework Assignment 2 🖥 **S2-6** ⓢⓟ<br>• Scissors<br>• Blank paper (or real game pawns)<br>• Pens or pencils<br>• Dice<br>• *Optional:* Computers<br>• Smart Board or whiteboard | • **Grade 6–8** Copy the Session 2 Journal Entries.<br>• **Grade 9–12** Copy the Session 2 Real-Life Story.<br>• Copy the Is It or Isn't It? game board.<br>• Copy and cut out the Is It or Isn't It? game cards.<br>• Cut the blank paper into small game pieces, or use real game pawns.<br>• Copy the Is It or Isn't It? Peer Leader Instructions.<br>• Gather dice.<br>• Copy Homework Assignment 2. |

Duplicating this page is illegal. Do not copy this material without written permission from the publisher.

| Session Title | Session Description | Materials Needed | Preparation Needed |
|---|---|---|---|
| **Session 3: How Does Cyberbullying Affect People?** | Through student journal entries or a real-life story and group discussion, students will understand the serious effects of cyberbullying. Students will also develop strategies to offer support to peers through the use of digital technologies. | • CD-ROM materials<br>• **Grade 6–8** Session 3 Journal Entries S3-1<br>• **Grade 9–12** Session 3 Real-Life Story S3-2<br>• Digital Support Game S3-3<br>• Homework Assignment 3 S3-4 (SP)<br>• Magazines or newspapers<br>• One sheet of poster board<br>• Scissors<br>• Glue | • **Grade 6–8** Copy the Session 3 Journal Entries.<br>• **Grade 9–12** Copy the Session 3 Real-Life Story.<br>• Copy the Digital Support Game.<br>• Copy Homework Assignment 3.<br>• Look through the magazines or newspapers to find and cut out pictures of the following: a person (could be a celebrity), a group of friends, a school, someone laughing, a key, and a house. Lightly glue the picture of the person in the middle of the poster board and glue the rest of the pictures around the person. Label each picture in this manner:<br>• Person = Self-Esteem<br>• Group of Friends = Friends<br>• School = School/Learning<br>• Laughing Person = Happiness<br>• Key = Safety<br>• House = Home/Family |

Duplicating this page is illegal. Do not copy this material without written permission from the publisher.

| Session Title | Session Description | Materials Needed | Preparation Needed |
|---|---|---|---|
| **Session 4: Why Do People Cyberbully Others?** | Through journal entries or a real-life story and small- and large-group discussions, students will understand why teens cyberbully others. Then through the creation of public service announcements (PSAs), students will take steps to prevent cyberbullying and take a stand against it. | • CD-ROM materials<br>• **Grade 6–8** Session 4 Journal Entries S4-1<br>• **Grade 9–12** Session 4 Real-Life Story S4-2<br>• Cyberbullying poster I-15<br>• PSA Planning Sheet S4-3<br>• Homework Assignment 4 S4-4 (SP)<br>• Your school's policy(ies) on bullying or cyber-bulling, if available<br>• Smart Board or whiteboard<br>• Materials for PSAs, such as poster board, video cameras, or digital recorders | • **Grade 6–8** Copy the Session 4 Journal Entries.<br>• **Grade 9–12** Copy the Session 4 Real-Life Story.<br>• Copy the PSA Planning Sheet.<br>• Copy Homework Assignment 4.<br>• Before class, check with your school administrator about what policy or policies are in place regarding cyberbullying and review the policies. If none are in place, maybe your class can lobby for some.<br>• Display the Cyberbullying poster. |

Duplicating this page is illegal. Do not copy this material without written permission from the publisher.

| Session Title | Session Description | Materials Needed | Preparation Needed |
|---|---|---|---|
| **Session 5: How Should You React to Cyberbullying?** | Through journal entries or a real-life story, small- and large-group discussions, and sample situations, students will learn what to do if someone cyberbullies them or another person. | • CD-ROM materials<br>  • **Grade 6–8** Session 5 Journal Entries 📄 **S5-1**<br>  • **Grade 9–12** Session 5 Real-Life Story 📄 **S5-2**<br>• Do First poster and handout 📄 **I-15, S5-3**<br>• Question Cube Template 📄 **S5-4**<br>• What Would You Do If...? situation sheets 📄 **S5-5**<br>• Homework Assignment 5 📄 **S5-6** (SP)<br>• Smart Board or whiteboard<br>• Your school's bullying/cyberbullying policy, if available<br>• Scissors<br>• Clear tape | • **Grade 6–8** Copy the Session 5 Journal Entries.<br>• **Grade 9–12** Copy the Session 5 Real-Life Story.<br>• Print out the Do First poster; enlarge and display it in your space.<br>• Copy the Do First handout.<br>• Copy, cut, and assemble the Question Cubes.<br>• Print out the What Would You Do If...? situation sheets, one set per small group. Select the situations for your classroom, cut them out, and have them ready for each peer leader.<br>• Copy Homework Assignment 5. |

Duplicating this page is illegal. Do not copy this material without written permission from the publisher.

| Session Title | Session Description | Materials Needed | Preparation Needed |
|---|---|---|---|
| **Session 6: Creating a Positive Social-Networking Site or App, Part I** | Through a small-group project, students will create plans for their own social-networking sites or apps that will promote safe and positive Internet use. | • CD-ROM materials<br>  • Facebook Statement of Rights and Responsibilities  S6-2<br>  • Social-Networking Site or App Planning Packet  S6-3<br>  • Facts of the Feature sheet  S6-4<br>  • **Grade 6–8** Session 6 Journal Entries  S6-1<br>• Smart Board or whiteboard | • Write the Facebook information on a whiteboard or display it on a Smart Board.<br>• Copy the Social-Networking Site or App Planning Packet.<br>• Copy the Facts of the Feature sheet.<br>• **Grade 6–8** Copy the Session 6 Journal Entries.<br>• Visit some social-networking sites so you are familiar with their format and content. |
| **Session 7: Creating a Positive Social-Networking Site or App, Part II** | Students will fill out a form to commit to helping stop cyberbullying and to explain what they will do if they are aware of cyberbullying situations. Students will also continue to work on their website/app project plans. | • CD-ROM materials<br>  • Cyber Solutions sheet  S7-1<br>• Social-Networking Site or App Planning Packet<br>• Materials for the project, including large paper or poster board, markers, and colored pencils<br>• *Optional:* Computers | • Copy the Cyber Solutions sheet.<br>• Gather project materials. |
| **Session 8: Creating a Positive Social-Networking Site or App, Part III** | Students will read one of their commitments to the class about how they will stop and/or prevent cyberbullying. They will also present their social-networking site/app project plans to the class. | • CD-ROM materials<br>  • Social-Networking Site or App Plan Presentation Score Sheet  S8-1<br>• *Optional:* Video camera to film the presentations | • Copy the Social-Networking Site or App Plan Presentation Score Sheet.<br>• *Optional:* Make sure the video camera is ready for filming.<br>• On your calendar, mark a date (one or two months from today) when you will give the Cyber Solutions sheets back to the students.<br>• If possible, invite a school administrator to listen to your students' presentations. |

Duplicating this page is illegal. Do not copy this material without written permission from the publisher.

## Cyberbullying Pre-test/Post-test

Name_____ Class Period_____

**Write your answers in the spaces provided.**

1. What is the definition of *bullying*?

_____

_____

_____

_____

2. List three roles people could play in an incidence of bullying.

a. _____

b. _____

c. _____

3. List three technologies that can be used in cyberbullying.

a. _____

b. _____

c. _____

Duplicating this page for personal or group use is permissible.

4. List two ways that cyberbullying differs from traditional bullying.

    a. _____

    b. _____

5. List two ways that being cyberbullied might affect someone your age.

    a. _____

    b. _____

6. List two reasons a person might cyberbully someone else.

    a. _____

    b. _____

7. List three things you could do if you were cyberbullied.

    a. _____

    b. _____

    c. _____

8. List three things that most social-networking sites don't allow.

    a. _____

    b. _____

    c. _____

Duplicating this page for personal or group use is permissible.

**Write "T" for True or "F" for False
on the line in front of each statement below.**

_____ 9. Only two people are involved in a bullying situation—the person who bullies and the person who is bullied.

_____ 10. Sending an embarrassing or insulting photo through email is cyberbullying.

_____ 11. Cyberbullying can only occur through the Internet.

_____ 12. Students who are cyberbullied often don't want to go to school.

_____ 13. Showing empathy means donating money to help those who are cyberbullied.

_____ 14. One reason people cyberbully others is because they think no one will find out who did it.

_____ 15. If cyberbullying happens outside of school, it is still a good idea to tell adults at school about it.

_____ 16. It's important to save the evidence if you are cyberbullied.

_____ 17. A good way to deal with cyberbullying is to retaliate immediately.

_____ 18. Social-networking sites cannot take any action against someone who is using the site to abuse or insult others.

Duplicating this page for personal or group use is permissible.

### Answers for the Pre-test/Post-test

1. *Bullying* is when someone repeatedly and on purpose says or does mean or hurtful things to another person who has a hard time defending himself or herself.

2. Possible answers include descriptions of these eight participants:

   • **Kids Who Bully** start the bullying and play a leader role.

   • **Followers** take an active part, but don't usually start it.

   • **Supporters** support the bullying but don't take an active role.

   • **Passive Supporters** like the bullying but don't show outward signs of support.

   • **Disengaged Onlookers** are aware of what is happening but may feel "It's none of my business."

   • **Possible Defenders** dislike the bullying and think they should help but do nothing.

   • **Defenders** dislike the bullying and help or try to help the person who is being bullied.

   • **Person Who Is Bullied.**

3. Possible answers include these technologies:

   • cell phones/text messages

   • Internet/computer

   • websites

   • email

   • instant messaging

4. Possible answers include these differences:

   • Cyberbullying can reach and involve many people much more quickly than traditional bullying.

Duplicating this page for personal or group use is permissible.

- People who might not bully someone face to face might cyberbully someone because they can't be seen and think they are anonymous.

- Traditional bullying usually involves an imbalance of power. Students who bully target others they think won't fight back. Because people who cyberbully think they are anonymous, they might not be more physically or socially powerful but can feel more powerful by using technology.

- Traditional forms of bullying can cause physical harm and psychological harm. In most cases, cyberbullying causes psychological harm.

- Traditional bullying is usually limited to the people in the immediate area where the bullying is taking place. Cyberbullying can reach many people immediately—and often the target is unaware of who these people are.

- Traditional bullying usually has a time and place, such as the school playground at recess. Cyberbullying can happen anytime and any place. For a while, the target may even be unaware that it is happening.

- It is usually apparent who is doing traditional bullying. It is often difficult to find out who is doing cyberbullying.

5. Teens who are cyberbullied can become depressed, anxious, nervous, and fearful, and may have low self-esteem, avoid going to school, do poorly in school, lose friends, have damaged reputations, and feel unsafe.

6. People may cyberbully for these reasons:

- They think they can be anonymous.

- They can't be seen.

- They don't have to see the other person's reactions.

- Everybody does it, so it's no big deal.

- They like making someone else feel bad.

- They think it is entertaining.

- They are seeking revenge.

Duplicating this page for personal or group use is permissible.

7. Possible answers include ignore it, block the sender, tell an adult, respond but don't retaliate, trace the sender, contact the Internet service provider or social-networking site, and save the evidence.

8. Possible answers include these:

- harmful, threatening, obscene, abusive, racist language

- content that harms minors in some way

- stalking behavior

- content that provides instructions for or promotion of illegal activities

- pornographic content of minors

- impersonating another user or person

- soliciting personal information for anyone under the age of eighteen

- providing a false age or birthday

9. False

10. True

11. False

12. True

13. False

14. True

15. True

16. True

17. False

18. False

Duplicating this page for personal or group use is permissible.

# The Sessions

## CYBERBULLYING
## SESSION 1

# What Is Bullying?

## Description

Through student journal entries or a real-life story, small- and large-group discussions, and word collages, students will define *bullying* and learn about the Bullying Circle diagram and rules against bullying.

## Learner Outcomes

By the end of this session, students will be able to

- define *bullying*.

- identify examples of bullying.

- identify the roles students play in the Bullying Circle.

- identify rules against bullying.

## Materials Needed

- ☐ CD-ROM materials:

  - Parent Letter 🗒 I-12 (SP)

  - Completed Why Should We Talk About Cyberbullying? peer leader handouts (completed during peer leader training) 🗒 I-10

**SESSION 1
AT A GLANCE**

Total Time: 50 minutes

*Part 1:*
Program
Introduction
*(5 minutes)*

*Part 2:*
Journal Entries/
Real-Life Story
and Discussion
*(20 minutes)*

*Part 3:*
Creating Anti-
Bullying Collages
and Posters
*(20 minutes)*

*Part 4:*
Conclusion
and Homework
Assignment
*(5 minutes)*

Duplicating this page is illegal. Do not copy this material without written permission from the publisher.

39

**TEACHER TIP**

*Make sure you read all the journal entries for sessions 1–6 before beginning the program. It is important that you know the flow of the story and the sequence of material as it is presented.*

- Session 1 Journal Entries  S1-1
- Session 1 Real-Life Story  S1-2
- The Bullying Circle diagram  S1-3
- The Four Anti-Bullying Rules poster  S1-4
- Homework Assignment 1  S1-5  (SP)

☐ Collage materials including the following:

- Poster board or large pieces of paper (one per small group of three to four students with one peer leader)

- Magazines

- Newspapers

- Scissors

- Glue or tape

- Markers and/or crayons

- Pens or pencils

☐ *Optional:* Smart Board or whiteboard

## Preparation Needed

1. Print out and send the Parent Letter home with each student prior to starting the program.

2. Print out the Session 1 Journal Entries, one set per student.

   Students will be working on the journal entries in their small groups. Each small group will work on a different character and all students in that small group will need a copy of that character's journal entry. However, you may wish to give all students a copy of all four journal entries to follow along as they are read aloud. You may

Duplicating this page is illegal. Do not copy this material without written permission from the publisher.

also want to have extra copies so that members of a small group could discuss a second character if they finish their work early.

**Grade 9–12**

3. Print out the Session 1 Real-Life Story, one copy per student.

4. Gather the collage materials.

5. Print out and make copies of Homework Assignment 1, one per student.

**TEACHER TIP**
*This lesson includes a lot of material to cover. You may want to watch your time closely or divide this into two class periods.*

6. Read through all of the journal entries for sessions 1–6, so you will know how the stories progress as the program continues.

7. Return the Why Should We Talk About Cyberbullying? handouts to their peer leader authors.

8. If you are using a Smart Board, make sure you have the Bullying Circle diagram and the Four Anti-Bullying Rules poster ready to go on your computer. If you are using a whiteboard, write these out for the students to see.

Duplicating this page is illegal. Do not copy this material without written permission from the publisher.

41

**SESSION**  **OUTLINE**

**PART 1**
5 minutes

▶ **Program Introduction**

The purpose of part 1 is to introduce the *Cyberbullying* curriculum to students and to get them thinking about why it is important to discuss the topic of bullying. The role of peer leaders will also be explained to the students.

1. Explain to the students:

   **Today we are starting a program about cyberbullying. How many of you have heard this term before? Some of you may already have or know someone who has experienced cyberbullying, while some of you may not know what it is. Over the next eight sessions, we will learn more about cyberbullying and what we can do to prevent it.**

   **One exciting thing about this program is that the students you chose to be peer leaders will be leading much of the time during our sessions.**

2. Introduce the peer leaders by having them stand. Call on each one to read his or her Why Should We Talk About Cyberbullying? statement.

3. Thank the peer leaders and ask the rest of the class:

   **Why do you think it is important for us to talk about cyberbullying? Why is it important even if it hasn't happened to you and you haven't cyberbullied anyone?**

   Allow time for students to respond between questions.

4. Summarize by saying:

Duplicating this page is illegal. Do not copy this material without written permission from the publisher.

Cyberbullying affects everyone, even if you haven't experienced it. You may be a part of cyberbullying even if you don't know it. For example, if you've forwarded an email or "liked" a comment that makes fun of someone to one or more friends, that is considered cyberbullying.

To understand what cyberbullying is, it helps to first learn more about what bullying is and how we can prevent it. This is what we will be talking about today.

Duplicating this page is illegal. Do not copy this material without written permission from the publisher.

**PART 2**
20 minutes

▶ **Journal Entries/Real-Life Story and Discussion**

The purpose of part 2 is to have students discuss examples of bullying. Through these discussions, they will define *bullying*, understand the Bullying Circle, and identify rules against bullying.

 S1-1  Grade 6–8

**Journal Entries**

**TEACHER TIP**

*An alternative to paper and pencil journal entries would be to post these on a blog or message board accessible only to you and your students. This will help extend the learning. Suggestions for online homework using these online journal entries are included at the end of this session.*

1. Introduce the journal entries by telling the students that although these entries are about fictional students, bullying instances like these happen to students every day. Hand out a set of Session 1 Journal Entries to each student.

2. Explain to the students:

   **We are going to start talking about cyberbullying by figuring out what bullying is and how students may be involved in it. We will read some journal entries from some students like you.**

**TEACHER TIP**

*You could also ask students to read the journal entries aloud. Be sure to choose students who can read expressively, or give the entries to them ahead of time so they are familiar with the material. You could also assign this reading to the peer leaders.*

3. After the journal entries have been read, divide the class into small groups and assign one peer leader to each small group. Designate an area in the room where each small group will meet. They will meet in the same area for every session of the program.

4. Explain to the students:

   **The small group you are now in will be the group you will stay with for this entire unit on cyberbullying prevention. You will meet in the same place every time. Each small group will be assigned one of the journal entries. The peer leader in your group will lead you in a discussion to talk about the questions about that entry, and then you will report back to the whole class.**

Duplicating this page is illegal. Do not copy this material without written permission from the publisher.

**TEACHER TIP**

*Decide on the size and makeup of the small groups based on how your students work together and how many students you think will be manageable for the peer leaders to direct. The younger the students (middle school, for example), the smaller the groups should be. If you are aware of students who have a history of bullying or being bullied, make sure they are not in the same group, so they feel comfortable talking about their experiences.*

5. Assign each small group one of the student characters. If there are more than four small groups, two groups can work on the journal entry of the same character.

6. Allow 7 to 10 minutes for small groups to discuss the questions for the character they are assigned.

7. When the groups are ready, call on the peer leaders to read aloud to the class their groups' answers to the questions. Call on all the groups who discussed the same character together so you can summarize their answers and add comments according to the suggestions below.

Here are some suggested comments you can use to summarize each journal entry:

### Character: Allie

Summarize by including these points:

**Definition of *bullying:* Bullying occurs when someone repeatedly and on purpose says or does mean or hurtful things to another person who has a hard time defending himself or herself** (Olweus et al. 2007, xii).

**Bullying is aggressive and unwanted behavior.**

**Bullying involves a pattern of behavior that is repeated over time.**

**Bullying involves an imbalance of power or strength. The power could be physical, emotional, social, or economic.**

**Teasing can be playful or friendly. But if it is degrading and offensive or if the teaser has been told to stop, it can become bullying if it continues.**

Duplicating this page is illegal. Do not copy this material without written permission from the publisher.

**TEACHER TIP**
*Throughout the curriculum as students report back about their discussions, you may need to guide or reframe their answers to correct misconceptions as they arise.*

*Character: J.T.*

Summarize by including these points:

**There are many different kinds of bullying:**

- **verbal bullying, such as name calling and making derogatory comments**

- **physical bullying, such as hitting, kicking, shoving, and spitting**

- **making threats or forcing someone to do something**

- **exclusion, which is leaving someone out or excluding them from a social group**

- **rumor spreading or lying**

- **theft and extortion of money or property, or damaging property**

- **racial bullying***

- **sexual harassment***

- **cyberbullying through the use of technology and Internet communication**

**Bullying can be direct or indirect. It can be to someone's face or it can be behind the person's back, such as spreading rumors about someone or sending text messages about someone to others.**

---

* These behaviors go beyond bullying and may be illegal.

Duplicating this page is illegal. Do not copy this material without written permission from the publisher.

*Character: Serena*

Summarize by including these points:

**These are the four rules to prevent bullying that are used in the *Olweus Bullying Prevention Program (OBPP)*** (Olweus et al. 2007, 52–56):*

- **We will not bully others. (Bullying is not acceptable.)**

- **We will try to help students who are bullied. (We can do this by finding an adult to help, defending the student who is bullied, or befriending a student who is bullied.)**

- **We will try to include students who are left out. (Students who are bullied are often excluded.)**

- **If we know that somebody is being bullied, we will tell an adult at school and an adult at home. (Telling is not snitching *[or use the term commonly used by your students]*; it is following the rule that no bullying is allowed and may prevent someone from being hurt either physically or emotionally. Telling takes courage.)**

Display the Four Anti-Bullying Rules poster.

*Character: Aaron*

Summarize by including these points:

**Everyone who sees or is involved in a bullying situation plays a part in it and is affected by it.**

**The roles people play in bullying situations depend on their attitudes (positive, neutral, or negative) and their actions or behaviors (joining in, watching, helping).**

---

*If you are already implementing *OBPP*, this discussion will be a review. If not, adopt these rules in your classroom, and encourage your administrators to consider adopting these rules schoolwide.

Duplicating this page is illegal. Do not copy this material without written permission from the publisher.

The different roles people play in bullying situations are called the **Bullying Circle** (Snyder et al. 2014, 17–18). **The Bullying Circle includes these participants:**

- **Kids Who Bully** start the bullying and play a leader role.

- **Person Who Is Bullied.**

- **Followers who take an active part, but don't usually start it.**

- **Supporters who support the bullying but don't take an active role.**

- **Passive Supporters who like the bullying but don't show outward signs of support.**

- **Disengaged Onlookers who are aware of what is happening but may feel "It's none of my business."**

- **Possible Defenders who dislike the bullying and think they should help but do nothing.**

- **Defenders who dislike the bullying and help or try to help the person who is being bullied.**

 S1-3

Show the Bullying Circle diagram as you talk about each role.

8. Summarize the activity by saying:

You have probably all found yourselves playing some role in a bullying situation—even if it was as a bystander. From now on, our class (*or* whole school) will start using these rules against bullying. This means that even if you just happen to be there, you should try to help. Don't be afraid to speak up if you see bullying behavior on school grounds. Telling an adult can prevent someone from getting into trouble or getting hurt. If you feel that you may be harmed by stepping in and helping, telling an adult can help stop the bullying too.

Duplicating this page is illegal. Do not copy this material without written permission from the publisher.

S1-2  **Real-Life Story**

1. When you introduce the real-life stories, let students know that each story is based on an actual event, but names and other facts have been changed and the points of view have been dramatized.

2. Hand out the Session 1 Real-Life Story to each small group.

3. Explain to the students:

**TEACHER TIP**
*An alternative to paper and pencil real-life stories would be to post these on a blog or message board accessible only to you and your students. This will help extend the learning. Suggestions for online homework using this real-life story are included at the end of this session.*

**We are going to start talking about cyberbullying by first figuring out what roles people play in bullying situations. Before we do that, let's refresh our memories on the definition of *bullying*:**

**Bullying occurs when someone repeatedly and on purpose says or does mean or hurtful things to another person who has a hard time defending himself or herself** (Olweus et al. 2007, xii).

**There are several parts people play in a traditional bullying incident. These roles make up the Bullying Circle:**

- **Kids Who Bully start the bullying and play a leader role.**

- **Person Who Is Bullied.**

- **Followers who take an active part, but don't usually start it.**

- **Supporters who support the bullying but don't take an active role.**

- **Passive Supporters who like the bullying but don't show outward signs of support.**

- **Disengaged Onlookers who are aware of what is happening but may feel "It's none of my business."**

Duplicating this page is illegal. Do not copy this material without written permission from the publisher.

- **Possible Defenders who dislike the bullying and think they should help but do nothing.**

- **Defenders who dislike the bullying and help or try to help the person who is being bullied.**

S1-3

Show the Bullying Circle diagram as you talk about each role.

**With the definition of *bullying* and the Bullying Circle in mind, let's read today's real-life story.**

At the beginning of each story is a paragraph describing the incident. Read the paragraph aloud to students. Most of the stories include at least two points of view. Ask for volunteers to each read one point of view aloud until all the views have been read.

**TEACHER TIP**

*Decide on the size and makeup of the small groups based on how your students work together and how many students you think will be manageable for the peer leaders to direct. If you are aware of students who have a history of bullying or being bullied, make sure they are not in the same group, so they feel comfortable talking about their experiences.*

4. After the real-life story has been read, divide the class into small groups and assign one peer leader to each small group. Designate an area in the room where each small group will meet. The groups will meet in the same areas for every session of the program.

5. Explain to the students:

**The small group you are now in will be the group you will stay with for this entire unit on cyberbullying prevention. You will meet in the same place every time. Each small group will receive a copy of the day's real-life story with some questions. The peer leader in your group will lead you in a discussion to talk about the questions, and then you will report back to the whole class.**

6. Allow 7 to 10 minutes for small groups to discuss the questions relating to the story.

7. After the allotted time, call the class back to order. Assign each group a question to answer first in front of the group to

Duplicating this page is illegal. Do not copy this material without written permission from the publisher.

**TEACHER TIP**
*Throughout the curriculum as students report back about their discussions, you may need to guide or reframe their answers to correct misconceptions as they arise.*

**TEACHER TIP**
Olweus *is pronounced Ol-vay-us.*

spark discussion. (If there are more groups than questions, double-up groups on a question and allow all of them to read their responses first.) After the designated group has given its answers, invite other groups to respond and give their answers. Some answers may be repeated, but this format will allow thoughtful discussion.

8. Explain to the students:

   **Bullying is so prevalent that there are prevention programs out there for schools to implement. One such program is the *Olweus Bullying Prevention Program*. Within this program is the opportunity and suggestion to implement these Four Anti-Bullying Rules:\***

   - **We will not bully others.**

   - **We will try to help students who are bullied.**

   - **We will try to include students who are left out.**

   - **If we know that somebody is being bullied, we will tell an adult at school and an adult at home.**

S1-4

   *Optional:* Display the Four Anti-Bullying Rules poster.

9. Summarize the activity by saying:

   **You have probably all found yourselves playing some role in a bullying situation—even if it was as a bystander. From now on, keep these rules in mind. Don't be afraid to speak up if you see some bullying behavior on school grounds. Our next activity will help us internalize these rules and help out another school at the same time.**

---

\*Alternate language if your school is already implementing *OBPP:*

**As you know, our school is implementing the *Olweus Bullying Prevention Program*. As part of this program, our school has adopted these Four Anti-Bullying Rules.**

Duplicating this page is illegal. Do not copy this material without written permission from the publisher.

**PART 3**
20 minutes

▶ **Creating Anti-Bullying Collages and Posters**

The purpose of part 3 is to help students remember and understand the rules to prevent bullying. Middle school students will create collages that will establish the classroom as a "no bullying allowed" environment. High school students will create posters of these rules to donate to an elementary school in the district.

Grade
6–8

**Collages**

**TEACHER TIP**
*Students can work on their collages or posters in their peer-led small groups or in pairs.*

1. Explain to the students:

   **The four rules to prevent bullying will become part of our class rules. To remember them and think about what they mean, you will be creating word collages about each rule.**

**TEACHER TIP**
*You should have magazines, newspapers, or other print materials available for students to use in their collages and posters. They can also use other art materials that are available, such as markers, colored pencils or pens, crayons, scissors, glue sticks, and colored paper.*

   Divide the class into groups. Assign each group one of the Four Anti-Bullying Rules. Also give each group a piece of paper or poster board. Leave the Four Anti-Bullying Rules poster displayed, so students can copy the rules onto their papers. Then have each group look through newspapers and magazines, cutting out words and phrases that apply to the rule or that are associated with the rule. The collages will be posted to remind students of these rules for the class.

2. Explain what other art materials could be used and that the materials should be shared among the groups or pairs.

3. Allow time for the groups or pairs to work on their collages. If time permits, have students show their collages to the rest of the class. When the collages are finished, post them in your classroom.

Duplicating this page is illegal. Do not copy this material without written permission from the publisher.

**Grade 9–12**    **Posters**

1. Explain to the students:

   **As you know, the four rules to prevent bullying are a huge part of the *Olweus Bullying Prevention Program.* This program is usually done in elementary and middle schools. But that doesn't mean that we can't keep these rules in mind as we go about our lives here in our high school. To help us remember them and to help students at the elementary schools in our district, we are going to create posters of each rule to donate to one of the elementary schools.**

   Split the class into four groups. Assign each group one of the Four Anti-Bullying Rules. Give each group a piece of poster board and art supplies.

**TEACHER TIP**
*Instead of creating posters with paper and glue, groups could create them on the computer and print them out.*

2. Have each group look through newspapers and magazines, cutting out letters, words, and pictures to create posters that state the rules.

3. Allow time for the groups to work on their posters. If time permits, have students show their posters to the rest of the class. When the posters are finished, donate them to an elementary school in your district.

Duplicating this page is illegal. Do not copy this material without written permission from the publisher.

**PART 4**
5 minutes

▶ **Conclusion and Homework Assignment**

1. Wrap up by inviting student volunteers to define *bullying* and the roles people play in the Bullying Circle.

**Today we learned what bullying is and how we can all be a part of it even if we're not the one who starts it. We're also trying to stop it by using rules to prevent bullying in our classroom.**

Call on students to repeat the rules against bullying:

- We will not bully others.

- We will try to help students who are bullied.

- We will try to include students who are left out.

- If we know that somebody is being bullied, we will tell an adult at school and an adult at home.

Wrap up by inviting student volunteers to define *bullying* and the roles people play in the Bullying Circle.

**After today's activities, we all have a better understanding of what bullying is and how harmful it can be. Although we are donating the posters you created to an elementary school, the rules we worked with are something we should keep in mind for how we conduct ourselves here at** (*insert name of your school*).

2. Explain:

**Next time we will begin to talk about cyberbullying, what it is, and what we can do about it.**

3. Hand out Homework Assignment 1. Explain to the students:

Duplicating this page is illegal. Do not copy this material without written permission from the publisher.

This homework assignment is for you to do with your parent or an adult you live with. If it is not possible for an adult you live with to do it with you, then another adult, like a relative or neighbor, could. If you have trouble finding an adult to work with, come and see me, and I will help you.

You will have five of these homework assignments during the program. Each one will have background information from the session for your parents or another adult to read through. It also has activities for you to do with that person, which will give you a chance to teach the adult what you learned and to hear what he or she thinks about it. These are the activities this week:

- The adult shares a bullying experience from his or her youth with you.

- You both look at some bullying prevention websites or do an Internet search for bullying stories together.

If you do not have access to the Internet, you can visit a library and do this assignment there. If this is not possible, look through newspapers and magazines for articles about bullying.

When you and the adult you are working with have finished the homework assignment, both of you need to sign the return slip on the last page and you will bring that part back. You will be graded on this assignment.

4. If you are posting the journal entries online, have students read through today's entries again and answer these questions online:

What, if any, bullying situations have you seen or been a part of at school that are like the ones described in the journal entries?

Duplicating this page is illegal. Do not copy this material without written permission from the publisher.

Caution students not to use names or too many details.

 If you are posting the real-life stories online, have students read through today's story again and answer this question online:

Why might popular students like Todd think that the bullying they are doing is not bullying but playing a joke or pulling a prank?

  5. Show the students where to put their homework slips.

6. Explain how students will be graded on this homework assignment.

7. Tell the students when the homework assignment will be due.

---

The definition of *bullying* and the Four Anti-Bullying Rules are from Olweus, Dan, Susan P. Limber, Vicki Crocker Flerx, Nancy Mullin, and Jane Riese. 2007. *Olweus Bullying Prevention Program: Teacher Guide.* Center City, MN: Hazelden Publishing. The Bullying Circle and roles are from Snyder, Marlene, Jane Riese, Susan P. Limber, Dan Olweus, and Stein Gorseth. 2014. *Olweus Bullying Prevention Program: Community Youth Organization Guide.* Center City, MN: Hazelden Publishing.

Duplicating this page is illegal. Do not copy this material without written permission from the publisher.

## CYBERBULLYING          SESSION 2

## What Is Cyberbullying?

### Description

Through student journal entries or a real-life story, small- and large-group discussions, and a board game, students will understand what cyberbullying is and is not, and the technologies used to cyberbully.

### Learner Outcomes

By the end of this session, students will be able to

- define *cyberbullying*.

- identify the technologies used in cyberbullying.

- identify cyberbullying situations.

### Materials Needed

☐ CD-ROM materials:

**Grade 6–8** • Session 2 Journal Entries ⬚ S2-1

**Grade 9–12** • Session 2 Real-Life Story ⬚ S2-2

- Is It or Isn't It? game board, one per small group ⬚ S2-4

- Is It or Isn't It? game cards, one set per small group ⬚ S2-5

- Is It or Isn't It? Peer Leader Instructions ⬚ S2-3

- Homework Assignment 2 ⬚ S2-6 (SP)

---

**SESSION 2 AT A GLANCE**

Total Time: 50 minutes

*Part 1:*
Journal Entries/ Real-Life Story and Discussion
*(25 minutes)*

*Part 2:*
Is It or Isn't It?
*(20 minutes)*

*Part 3:*
Conclusion and Homework Assignment
*(5 minutes)*

**TEACHER TIP**
*Before teaching this session, be sure to read the "Introduction to Cyberbullying" (pages 11–18) and go through the Teacher Training Presentation on the CD-ROM.* ⬚ I-14

---

Duplicating this page is illegal. Do not copy this material without written permission from the publisher.

☐ Scissors

☐ Blank paper, or real game pawns, one per student

☐ Pens or pencils

☐ Dice, one die per small group

☐ *Optional:* Computers

☐ Smart Board or whiteboard

## Preparation Needed

1. Print out the Session 2 Journal Entries, one set per student.

   Students will be working on the journal entries in their small groups. Each small group will work on a different character and all students in that small group will need a copy of that character's journal entry. However, you may wish to give all students a copy of all four journal entries to follow along as they are read aloud. You may also want to have extra copies so that members of a small group could discuss a second character if they finish their work early.

2. Print out the Session 2 Real-Life Story, one copy per student.

3. Print out the Is It or Isn't It? game board, one board per group.

4. Print and cut out the Is It or Isn't It? game cards, one set per group.

**TEACHER TIP**
*This lesson includes a lot to cover. Be mindful of your time or divide this lesson into two class periods.*

5. Cut the blank paper into small game pieces, or use real game pawns, one per student.

6. Print out the Is It or Isn't It? Peer Leader Instructions, one for each peer leader.

7. Gather dice.

8. Print out Homework Assignment 2, one copy per student.

Duplicating this page is illegal. Do not copy this material without written permission from the publisher.

## SESSION  2 OUTLINE

**PART 1**
25 minutes

▶ **Journal Entries/Real-Life Story and Discussion**

The purpose of part 1 is to have students discuss examples of cyberbullying to understand what cyberbullying is and what technologies can be used to cyberbully.

 S2-1  Grade 6–8

**TEACHER TIP**
*Extend the lesson by having students keep their own journals about cyberbullying. These journals should be graded based on completion of the assignment rather than content. It is important that students know the journals will be turned in and the teacher will read them. If students wish to write about specific incidents that they want to keep confidential, they should not use names of students involved.*

**Journal Entries**

1. Explain to the students:

   **Last session we talked about bullying. What are some examples of bullying?**

   Allow time for students to respond.

   **Now that we know more about what bullying is, we're going to learn what cyberbullying is. So that we don't get confused, we're going to call it *traditional bullying* when we talk about the kind of bullying that does not involve computers or cell phones, which we call *technology*. We'll use the term *cyberbullying* when technology is involved.**

   **You might already know of examples of cyberbullying, but you just don't realize it. Sadly, there are many ways to use technology in a harmful way. As you read about Allie, J.T., Serena, and Aaron, think about anything that you have heard about or gone through that might be similar to what happened with them.**

2. Hand out the Session 2 Journal Entries to the class. Read the journal entries aloud or have students read them aloud as the rest of the class follows along.

Duplicating this page is illegal. Do not copy this material without written permission from the publisher.

**TEACHER TIP**

*An alternative to paper and pencil journal entries would be to post these on a blog or message board accessible only to you and your students. This will help extend the learning. Suggestions for online homework for these journal entries are included at the end of this session.*

3. After the journal entries have been read, divide the class into the same peer-led small groups they were in last session and have them go to their designated areas in the classroom.

Assign one of the Session 2 Journal Entries to each group, making sure each group has a different character than the one it worked on last time. If there are more than four small groups, two groups can work on the journal entry of the same character.

4. Allow 7 to 10 minutes for small groups to discuss the questions for the characters they are assigned.

**TEACHER TIP**

*If one group finishes its discussion before the others, those students could work on the discussion questions of a second character.*

5. Before the groups are called on to report to the class, make a chart on the Smart Board or whiteboard with the following headings:

Traditional bullying is...        Cyberbullying is...

When the students report back to the class, fill in the chart with characteristics of traditional bullying under the heading "Traditional bullying is..." and examples of cyberbullying under the heading "Cyberbullying is...." Keep in mind that many of the characteristics under each heading will be the same.

**TEACHER TIP**

*Throughout the curriculum as students report back about their discussions, you may need to guide or reframe their answers to correct misconceptions as they arise.*

6. When the groups are ready, call on the peer leaders to read aloud to the class their groups' answers to the questions. Call on all the groups who discussed the same character together. Fill in the chart as the students read their answers.

 S2-2   Grade 9–12    **Real-Life Story**

1. Explain to the students:

   **Last session, we talked about bullying. What are some examples of bullying?**

  Duplicating this page is illegal. Do not copy this material without written permission from the publisher.

Allow time for students to respond.

**Now that we have a clearer understanding of what bullying is, we can start talking about what cyberbullying is. So that we don't confuse the two, we're going to use the term *traditional bullying* when we refer to the kind of bullying that does not involve technology. We'll use the term *cyberbullying* when technology is involved.**

**You might already know of examples of cyberbullying, but you just don't realize it. Unfortunately, there are many ways to use technology in a negative way. As you read today's real-life story, think of any similar examples that you know about or may have even experienced.**

**TEACHER TIP**
*An alternative to paper and pencil real-life stories would be to post these on a blog or message board accessible only to you and your students. This will help extend the learning. Suggestions for online homework involving this real-life story are included at the end of this session.*

2. Hand out the Session 2 Real-Life Story to the class. At the beginning of the story is a paragraph describing the incident. Read the paragraph aloud. Then choose students or ask for volunteers to read the other sections of the story aloud.

3. After the real-life story has been read, divide the class into the same peer-led small groups and have them go to their designated areas in the classroom.

4. Allow 7 to 10 minutes for small groups to discuss the questions related to the story.

5. Before the groups are called on to report to the class, make a chart on the Smart Board or whiteboard with the following headings:

Traditional bullying is...        Cyberbullying is...

When the students report back to the class, fill in the chart with characteristics of traditional bullying under the heading "Traditional bullying is..." and examples of cyberbullying under the heading "Cyberbullying is...."

Duplicating this page is illegal. Do not copy this material without written permission from the publisher.

Keep in mind that many of the characteristics under each heading will be the same.

**TEACHER TIP**
*Throughout the curriculum as students report back about their discussions, you may need to guide or reframe their answers to correct misconceptions as they arise.*

6. When the groups are ready, call the class back to order. Assign each group a question to answer first in front of the group to spark discussion. (If there are more groups than questions, double-up groups on a question and allow all of the groups to read their responses before discussion.) After the designated group has given its answers, invite other groups to respond and give their answers. Some answers may be repeated, but this format allows thoughtful discussion.

Grade
9–12    **Chart Summary**

1. After all of the groups have reported back, summarize the information on the right side of the chart by including these examples and talking points:

**Cyberbullying can involve the following** (Kowalski, Limber, and Agatston 2012):

- sending mean or offensive messages repeatedly through emails, instant messaging, text messages, cell phone messages, chat room posts, or Facebook or Instagram postings

- playing an online game and ruining the game for others on purpose

- sending put-downs and insults through emails or text messages

- humiliating people through technology, for example, posting information that is not true, altering photos in an offensive way, or making fun of someone through statements, photos, or songs

    Duplicating this page is illegal. Do not copy this material without written permission from the publisher.

- creating websites designed to humiliate or embarrass others (such as sites where you rate others), or using anonymous question-and-answer social-networking sites to ask mean questions or post anonymous threats

- sending messages as though they are from someone else, which usually happens by using the targeted student's password and sending mean, offensive, or inappropriate messages or comments so that the receiver thinks the targeted student sent them

- sharing personal, often embarrassing, information about someone that the person would not want shared by forwarding an email or a photo to others

- tricking someone into sharing personal information and then telling others about it through emails or text messaging

- leaving someone out of a group by taking the person off friends lists or leaving the person out of password-protected sites

- hitting or hurting someone while photographing or video-taping the person, usually with a cell phone, and then sending the photos or videos to others for amusement

- sending threats intending to harm someone or encouraging the person to commit suicide—which should be reported to an adult immediately

2. Reread the definition of *bullying* below and ask the students to come up with their own definition of *cyberbullying*:

**Bullying occurs when someone repeatedly and on purpose says or does mean or hurtful things to another person who has a hard time defending himself or herself** (Olweus et al. 2007, xii).

3. Summarize how traditional bullying and cyberbullying are alike and different by including these points:

Duplicating this page is illegal. Do not copy this material without written permission from the publisher.

- Both traditional bullying and cyberbullying are very harmful.

- Cyberbullying can reach and involve many people very quickly.

- People who might not bully someone face to face might cyberbully someone because they can't be seen and think they are anonymous.

- Traditional bullying involves an imbalance of power. The student who bullies often targets someone he or she thinks won't fight back. Because those who cyberbully think they can be anonymous, they might not really be more physically or socially powerful, but they can feel powerful by using technology.

- Traditional forms of bullying can cause physical harm and psychological harm. In most cases, cyberbullying causes psychological harm.

- Traditional bullying is usually limited to the people in the immediate area where the bullying is taking place. Cyberbullying can reach many people immediately—and often the student who is targeted doesn't know who is doing it.

- Traditional bullying usually has a time and place, such as during lunch on school grounds. Cyberbullying can happen anytime and anyplace. The targeted student may even be unaware that it is happening for a while.

- It is usually apparent who is doing traditional bullying. It is often difficult to find out who is cyberbullying.

- Both traditional bullying and cyberbullying are not allowed at our school or in our classroom.

Ask students to describe examples of cyberbullying that they know about without using names or giving too many details.

Duplicating this page is illegal. Do not copy this material without written permission from the publisher.

## PART 2
20 minutes

S2-3 through S2-5

**TEACHER TIP**

*It is recommended that you review the game cards before playing the game in class to make sure all the cards are appropriate for your students' age level.*

▶ **Is It or Isn't It?**

The purpose of part 2 is for students to identify cyberbullying situations and to understand why these situations are considered cyberbullying and not just an online exchange or joke.

*Option 1:* Play the paper version of the game.

1. Explain:

   **We will now play a game in your small groups to help you identify what kinds of situations and online communications could be considered cyberbullying. Sometimes it's hard to tell. What you think is a joke might not be funny to someone else.**

2. Explain the directions of the game:

   **I will give each small group a game board, game pawns, a die, and game cards. Each group's peer leader will have the game directions.**

   **Each player will shake the die and move the number of spaces shown on the die. The player will then do whatever it says on the space where the pawn lands.**

   **If the player lands on a space that reads "Is It or Isn't It?" the peer leader will draw a card and read a situation to the player. The player will give two reasons they think that situation is or isn't cyberbullying.**

   **The peer leader will then read the answer from the bottom of the card. If the player is correct, he or she will move ahead two spaces. If incorrect, the player will not move. If the player gives a reason that isn't included on the card, the group can vote on the appropriateness of the reason. When it is the peer leader's turn, the peer leader will ask another player to read the card and the answer.**

Duplicating this page is illegal. Do not copy this material without written permission from the publisher.

**It's true that some situations might not be cyberbullying. But keep in mind that if someone sends you a message and you're not sure how to take it because you can't see the person's face, you need to clarify the message with that person to find out what was really meant.**

**The winner is the player who reaches the finish line first.**

3. Give the small groups their game materials. Give a game pawn or piece to each student. If using paper, have each student write his or her name on the game piece.

4. Allow 10 to 15 minutes to play the game.

Remove and do not play the cards that are *not* appropriate examples of cyberbullying for this age level.

*Option 2:* If you have access to a computer, you might want to invite the students to create and play an online version of this game instead of using the paper game.

Duplicating this page is illegal. Do not copy this material without written permission from the publisher.

| **PART 3**<br>5 minutes | ▶ **Conclusion and Homework Assignment** |

1. Explain:

   **You now have a good idea of what cyberbullying is and how harmful it can be. What are some ways that people can be cyberbullied?**

   Possible answers include repeatedly sending mean or offensive emails, chats, and/or texts; posting embarrassing information about someone else on a website; leaving someone out of a group or friends list; and sending messages as though they were from someone else.

   **Cyberbullying is not a joke or just something that everybody does. It's something to take seriously.**

   **What is something you learned today about cyberbullying that you had not realized before?**

   Allow several students to answer this question.

2. Summarize by saying:

   **It's important that everyone understands what cyberbullying is and how harmful it can be. Share what you learned today with a friend.**

 S2-6 (SP)

3. Hand out Homework Assignment 2. Explain to the students:

   **This homework assignment is for you to do with your parent or an adult you live with. If it is not possible for an adult you live with to do it with you, then another adult, such as a relative or neighbor, could. If you have trouble finding an adult to work with, come and see me, and I will help you. These are the activities for this week:**

Duplicating this page is illegal. Do not copy this material without written permission from the publisher.

• There is some information for the adult to read.

• You both take the True or False? Technology Quiz to see who knows more and what you can learn from each other.

**When you and the adult you are working with have completed the homework assignment, both of you need to sign the return slip at the bottom of the sheet and you will bring that part back to class. You will be graded on this assignment.**

 If you are posting the journal entries online, have students read through today's entries again and answer these questions online:

Which do you think would be harder, being cyberbullied or being the friend who is unable to help the person being cyberbullied? Why?

 If you are posting the real-life stories online, have students read through today's story again and answer these questions online:

Have you ever been or known someone who has been excluded from your online community? What happened? How was the situation resolved?

  4. Show the students where to put their homework slips.

5. Explain how students will be graded on this homework assignment.

6. Tell the students when the homework assignment will be due.

Duplicating this page is illegal. Do not copy this material without written permission from the publisher.

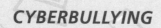

## *CYBERBULLYING*

## *SESSION 3*

# How Does Cyberbullying Affect People?

## Description

Through student journal entries or a real-life story and group discussion, students will understand the serious effects of cyberbullying. Students will also develop strategies to offer support to peers through the use of digital technologies.

## Learner Outcomes

By the end of this session, students will be able to

- identify the effects of cyberbullying on the student who is bullied, on bystanders, and on the students who bully.

- identify how to use technology in a positive way.

## Materials Needed

☐ CD-ROM materials:

**Grade 6–8**
- Session 3 Journal Entries 🖥 S3-1

**Grade 9–12**
- Session 3 Real-Life Story 🖥 S3-2

- Digital Support Game 🖥 S3-3

- Homework Assignment 3 🖥 S3-4 (SP)

☐ Magazines or newspapers

☐ One sheet of poster board

### SESSION 3 AT A GLANCE

**Total Time: 50 minutes**

*Part 1:*
Journal Entries/
Real-Life Story
and Discussion
*(15 minutes)*

*Part 2:*
Understanding
Empathy
*(15 minutes)*

*Part 3:*
Digital Support
Game
*(15 minutes)*

*Part 4:*
Conclusion
and Homework
Assignment
*(5 minutes)*

Duplicating this page is illegal. Do not copy this material without written permission from the publisher.

☐ Scissors

☐ Glue

## Preparation Needed

 1. Print out the Session 3 Journal Entries, one set per student.

Students will be working on the journal entries in their small groups. Each small group will work on a different character and all students in that small group will need a copy of that character's journal entry. However, you may wish to give all students a copy of all four journal entries to follow along as they are read aloud. You may also want to have extra copies so that members of a small group could discuss a second character if they finish their work early.

 2. Print out the Session 3 Real-Life Story, one copy per student.

3. Print out the Digital Support Game, one copy per small group.

4. Print out Homework Assignment 3, one copy per student.

5. Look through the magazines or newspapers to find and cut out pictures of the following: a person (could be a celebrity), a group of friends, a school, someone laughing, a key, and a house. Lightly glue the picture of the person in the middle of the poster board and glue the rest of the pictures around the person. Label the pictures in this manner:

| Image | Label |
| --- | --- |
| Person | Self-Esteem |
| Group of Friends | Friends |
| School | School/Learning |
| Laughing Person | Happiness |
| Key | Safety |
| House | Home/Family |

Duplicating this page is illegal. Do not copy this material without written permission from the publisher.

**S E S S I O N  3  O U T L I N E**

---

**PART 1**
15 minutes

▶ **Journal Entries/Real-Life Story and Discussion**

The purpose of part 1 is to have students understand how cyberbullying affects all the players in the Bullying Circle.

 S3-1   Grade 6–8

**Journal Entries**

1. Explain to the students:

   **During the last session, we learned what cyberbullying is. Who can refresh our memories as to what it is?**

   Allow time for students to respond.

   **We also started talking about how it can affect the person who is being cyberbullied. What do you think is happening to Allie from the Session 2 Journal Entries? Would this be cyberbullying?**

**TEACHER TIP**

*An alternative to paper and pencil journal entries would be to post these on a blog or message board accessible only to you and your students. This will help extend the learning. Suggestions for online homework related to these journal entries are included at the end of this session.*

2. Hand out the Session 3 Journal Entries to the class. Read the journal entries or have students read them aloud as the rest of the class follows along.

3. After the journal entries have been read, divide the class into the peer-led small groups and have them go to their designated areas in the classroom.

   Assign journal entry characters to each small group, making sure each group has a different character than the one it worked on last time. If there are more than four small groups, two groups can work on the journal entry of the same character.

Duplicating this page is illegal. Do not copy this material without written permission from the publisher.

**TEACHER TIP**

*If one group finishes its discussion before the others, those students could work on the discussion questions of a second character.*

4. Allow 7 to 10 minutes for small groups to discuss the questions for the characters they are assigned.

5. When the groups are ready, call on the peer leaders to read aloud to the class their groups' answers to the questions. Call on all of the groups who discussed the same character together. As students report back about their discussions, you may need to guide or reframe their answers to correct misconceptions as they arise.

 S3-2  **Grade 9–12**

**Real-Life Story**

1. Explain to the students:

   **During the last session, we learned what cyberbullying is. Who can refresh our memories as to what it is?**

   Allow time for students to respond.

   **We also started talking about how it can affect the person who is being cyberbullied. As we read today's real-life story, think of how all of the students involved might be affected.**

**TEACHER TIP**

*An alternative to paper and pencil real-life stories would be to post these on a blog or message board accessible only to you and your students. This will help extend the learning. Suggestions for online homework related to the real-life story are included at the end of this session.*

2. Hand out the Session 3 Real-Life Story to the class. At the beginning of the story is a paragraph describing the incident. Read the paragraph aloud. Choose students or ask for volunteers to read the other sections of the story aloud.

3. After the real-life story has been read, divide the class into the same peer-led small groups and have them go to their designated areas in the classroom.

4. Allow 7 to 10 minutes for groups to discuss the questions related to the story.

5. When the groups are ready, call the class back to order. Assign each group a question to answer first in front of the entire group to spark discussion. (If there are more groups

Duplicating this page is illegal. Do not copy this material without written permission from the publisher.

than questions, double-up groups on a question and allow all of them to read their responses before discussing.) After the designated group has given its answers, invite other groups to respond and give their answers. Some answers may be repeated, but this format allows thoughtful discussion.

## Discussion Summary

1. Summarize by saying:

   **Everyone has the right to live his or her life without being bullied or harassed by someone else. It is important to understand that even if someone cyberbullies another person as a joke, it may not be a joke to the person who is being bullied.**

   **A common excuse is "I was only kidding." This excuse will not be accepted here, especially if the behavior harms the person it was meant for. The most important thing we should think about is how the bullied student is affected. This is where our concern should be.**

   **Cyberbullying can be so devastating that sometimes students have become depressed as a result, whether or not someone was "only kidding." Some students who have been cyberbullied have even died by suicide.**

   **Cyberbullying can also affect other people in the Bullying Circle. People who see it happening to others might be afraid it will happen to them. Some might feel pressured to join in when they don't want to. A school environment in which cyberbullying or any kind of bullying is taking place is not one that feels like a safe, friendly community.**

   **Those students who bully and are allowed to continue their behavior are also affected. As they get older, these students are more likely to get into other types of trouble and even commit crimes.**

Duplicating this page is illegal. Do not copy this material without written permission from the publisher.

**PART 2**
15 minutes

▶ **Understanding Empathy**

The purpose of this activity is to have students understand what empathy is and to think about what it would be like to be cyberbullied.

1. Explain:

   **You have heard many examples of cyberbullying so far. Now we are going to look at some things that are important to people your age and see how these things might be affected if you were cyberbullied.**

2. Display the prepared poster board.

**TEACHER TIP**
*Some questions may not be appropriate for your class or grade level. Use your discretion about which questions to ask.*

3. Ask the questions below to get students thinking about how all these things would be affected if they were cyberbullied. Ask at least three questions for each category. As the students talk about the negative effects, gradually tear that image off the poster. At the end of the discussion, there should be nothing left of the pictures—only the labels should remain.

*Self-Esteem*

- How might being cyberbullied affect how you feel about yourself?

- How would you feel about yourself if someone you knew were sending you mean messages?

- How would you feel if you were getting hurtful emails or text messages and you didn't know who sent them?

Duplicating this page is illegal. Do not copy this material without written permission from the publisher.

### Friends

- How would you feel about your friends if they were sending nasty text messages about you?

- How would you feel about your friends if they were excluding you?

- How would you feel about your friends if they were sharing personal information about you?

- How would you feel about your friends if you didn't know who was bullying you?

### School/Learning

- How would you feel if everyone at school saw a website that made fun of you?

- How would you feel if someone sent an embarrassing or insulting picture of you electronically to the whole school?

- How would you feel about going to school if your name were on a web page where people made mean comments about you?

- Why could being cyberbullied affect someone's grades and how well the person does in school?

### Happiness

- How might being cyberbullied affect how happy you are?

- Why might people who are cyberbullied feel depressed?

- Why might people who are cyberbullied feel anxious or nervous?

Duplicating this page is illegal. Do not copy this material without written permission from the publisher.

*Safety*

- How would you feel if someone anonymous was sending you pornographic photos?

- How safe would you feel if you kept getting text messages making fun of your weight or height or some aspect of your appearance?

- How much could you trust people at school if you didn't know who was pretending to be you and making comments on other people's profiles?

- How would you feel if you got hate messages referring to your sexuality?

- How would you feel if you got hate messages referring to your race?

*Home/Family*

- How would your interaction with your family members be affected if you were being cyberbullied and were afraid to or didn't want to tell them?

- How would your family react if you were moody and depressed or sad?

- How would your family feel if they viewed a social-networking site with negative or nasty comments posted about you on the site?

4. After the pictures have been ripped off the poster board, explain:

**Many teens who are cyberbullied would like to disappear, just like the pictures did. They feel so bad that they don't want to go to school or be with other teens because their reputations have been damaged.**

Duplicating this page is illegal. Do not copy this material without written permission from the publisher.

5. Ask if anyone knows what the word *empathy* means. Allow several students to try to explain the definition.

6. Then summarize their suggestions and provide this definition:

   **Empathy means understanding how someone else feels in a certain situation.**

7. Explain:

   **If you can empathize as you just did, then you can understand how harmful cyberbullying can be. Even if you think it's just a joke, think about how the other person will feel first.**

Duplicating this page is illegal. Do not copy this material without written permission from the publisher.

**PART 3**
15 minutes

▶ **Digital Support Game**

The purpose of part 3 is to help students build empathy and caring feelings toward others by using cyber technology in a positive way.

1. Explain:

   **Now that we have talked about all the negative effects of cyberbullying, let's think about the ways we can have positive interactions using technology. Just as negative messages can be hurtful, positive messages of support can encourage and validate us.**

   Invite students to share some examples of positive texts or messages.

   **Today you will have a chance to come up with some examples of texts and messages for using social media in positive and supportive ways. Each small group will be challenged to come up with at least five ideas. I will collect all your ideas at the end of class and make a list to hand out to everyone, so you can use these positive ideas to create a positive online climate.**

2. Have students rejoin their peer-led groups. Give each peer leader a Digital Support Game to fill out with his or her group.

3. Explain:

   **Each peer leader should write the new examples in the left-hand column on the sheet and their platforms (e.g., text, Facebook, Instagram) in the right-hand column.**

Duplicating this page is illegal. Do not copy this material without written permission from the publisher.

**Remember, these messages can only be positive. Here's an example:**

**I know you're nervous about today. Good luck!**

4. Allow approximately 10 minutes for the groups to work.

5. When the groups have finished, ask the peer leaders to share some of their groups' examples, as time permits.

6. Collect the sheets and combine the examples into one list to give students during your next session. Encourage students to use these new positive ideas when communicating with each other.

Duplicating this page is illegal. Do not copy this material without written permission from the publisher.

**PART 4**
5 minutes

▶ **Conclusion and Homework Assignment**

1. Explain:

Invite student volunteers to explain the definition of *empathy* and some of the effects that cyberbullying has on those involved.

**Technology can help us do things faster, easier, and sometimes better. But if it's abused, it can have serious consequences. Remember the new supportive ways to use social media and share them with your friends.**

 S3-4 (SP)

2. Hand out Homework Assignment 3. Explain to the students:

**This homework assignment is for you to do with your parent or an adult you live with. If it is not possible for an adult you live with to do it with you, then another adult, such as a relative or neighbor, could. If you have trouble finding an adult to work with, come and see me, and I will help you. These are the activities this week:**

- **The adult has some information to read.**

- **You both will go through the ABCs of Cyberbullying Prevention, which will give you ideas about ways to prevent or stop cyberbullying.**

**When you and the adult you are working with have completed the homework assignment, both of you need to sign the return slip at the bottom of the sheet and you need to bring that part back.**

Grade
6–8

If you are posting the journal entries online, have students read through today's entries again and answer this question online:

How is what is happening to Allie like what is happening to Mrs. Vargo?

Duplicating this page is illegal. Do not copy this material without written permission from the publisher.

If you are posting the real-life stories online, have students read through today's story again and answer this question online:

Why might some people think that watching and forwarding links to this video is *not* cyberbullying?

3. Show the students where to put their homework slips.

4. Explain how students will be graded on this homework assignment.

5. Tell the students when the homework assignment will be due.

Duplicating this page is illegal. Do not copy this material without written permission from the publisher.

81

# CYBERBULLYING

# SESSION 4

## Why Do People Cyberbully Others?

### Description

Through journal entries or a real-life story and small- and large-group discussions, students will understand why teens cyberbully others. Then through the creation of public service announcements (PSAs), students will take steps to prevent cyberbullying and take a stand against it.

### Learner Outcomes

By the end of this session, students will be able to

- identify reasons people think they can cyberbully others.

- state why they think cyberbullying is unacceptable.

### Materials Needed

☐ CD-ROM materials:

- Session 4 Journal Entries 📄 S4-1

- Session 4 Real-Life Story 📄 S4-2

- Cyberbullying poster 📄 I-15

- PSA Planning Sheet 📄 S4-3

- Homework Assignment 4 📄 S4-4 (SP)

## SESSION 4 AT A GLANCE

Total Time: 50 minutes

*Part 1:*
Journal Entries/
Real-Life Story
and Discussion
*(25 minutes)*

*Part 2:*
Stop Cyberbullying
*(20 minutes)*

*Part 3:*
Conclusion
and Homework
Assignment
*(5 minutes)*

Duplicating this page is illegal. Do not copy this material without written permission from the publisher.

☐ Your school's policy(ies) on bullying or cyberbullying, if available

☐ Smart Board or whiteboard

☐ Materials for PSAs, such as poster board, video cameras, or digital recorders, depending on the type of PSAs students will be doing

## Preparation Needed

1. Print out the Session 4 Journal Entries, one set per student.

   Students will be working on the journal entries in their small groups. Each small group will work on a different character and all students in that small group will need a copy of that character's journal entry. However, you may wish to give all students a copy of all four journal entries to follow along as they are read aloud. You may also want to have extra copies so that members of a small group could discuss a second character if they finish their work early.

2. Print out the Session 4 Real-Life Story, one copy per student.

3. Print out the PSA Planning Sheet, one copy per small group.

4. Print out Homework Assignment 4, one copy per student.

5. Before class, check with your school administrator about what policy or policies are in place regarding cyberbullying and review the policies. If none are in place, maybe your class can lobby for some.

6. Display the Cyberbullying poster.

**TEACHER TIP**
*This lesson includes a lot of content to cover. Be mindful of your time or divide the session into two class periods.*

Duplicating this page is illegal. Do not copy this material without written permission from the publisher.

**PART 1**
25 minutes

▶ **Journal Entries/Real-Life Story and Discussion**

The purpose of part 1 is to give students an understanding of why people cyberbully others and why they think they can get away with it.

 S4-1    Grade 6–8

**Journal Entries**

1. Explain to the students:

   **During the last session, we talked about the effects of cyberbullying, especially on the person who is being cyberbullied. What are some of these possible effects?**

   Allow several students to respond.

   **Why do you think anybody would do something so mean that could cause so much pain to someone else? That's what Allie, J.T., Serena, and Aaron talk about in their journal entries today.**

2. Hand out the Session 4 Journal Entries to the class. Read the journal entries or have students read them aloud as the rest of the class follows along.

3. After the journal entries have been read, divide the class into the same peer-led small groups and have them go to their designated areas in the classroom.

4. Assign one character in the journal entries to each small group, making sure each group has a different character than the one it worked on last time. If there are more than four small groups, two groups can work on the journal entry of the same character.

**TEACHER TIP**
*An alternative to paper and pencil journal entries would be to post these on a blog or message board accessible only to you and your students. This will help extend the learning. Suggestions for online homework related to these journal entries are included at the end of this session.*

Duplicating this page is illegal. Do not copy this material without written permission from the publisher.

**TEACHER TIP**

*If one group finishes its discussion before the others, those students could work on the discussion questions of a second character.*

5. Allow 7 to 10 minutes for small groups to discuss the questions related to the characters they are assigned.

6. When the groups are ready, call on the peer leaders to read aloud to the class their groups' answers to the questions. Call on all of the groups who discussed the same character together. As the students report back, make a list on a whiteboard or Smart Board of the reasons people cyberbully when it is such a mean thing to do.

 S4-2

## Real-Life Story

1. Explain to the students:

   **During the last session, we talked about the effects of cyber-bullying, especially on the person who is being cyberbullied. What are some of these possible effects?**

   Allow several students to respond.

   **Why do you think anybody would do something so mean that could cause so much pain to someone else? We will explore that question in our real-life story today.**

**TEACHER TIP**

*An alternative to paper and pencil real-life stories would be to post these on a blog or message board accessible only to you and your students. This will help extend the learning. Suggestions for online homework related to the real-life story are included at the end of this session.*

2. Hand out the Session 4 Real-Life Story to the class. At the beginning of the story is a paragraph describing the incident. Read the paragraph aloud. Then choose a student or ask for a volunteer to read the rest of the story aloud.

3. After the real-life story has been read, divide the class into the same peer-led small groups and have them go to their designated areas in the classroom.

4. Allow 7 to 10 minutes for small groups to discuss the questions related to this story.

 Duplicating this page is illegal. Do not copy this material without written permission from the publisher.

5. When the groups are ready, call the class back to order. Assign each group a question to answer first in front of the group to spark discussion. (If there are more groups than questions, double-up groups on a question and allow all of them to read their responses before discussion.) After the designated group has given its answers, invite other groups to respond and give their answers. Some answers may be repeated, but this format allows thoughtful discussion.

As the students report back, make a list on a whiteboard or Smart Board of the reasons people cyberbully when it is such a mean thing to do.

### Discussion Summary

1. Summarize students' answers by including these points:

**People may cyberbully because**

- **they think people won't know who they are; they can be anonymous.**

- **they can't be seen.**

- **they don't have to see the other person's reactions.**

- **they think everybody does it, so it's no big deal.**

- **they like making someone else feel bad.**

**Even though many people who cyberbully think no one will know they did it, people are never as anonymous online as they believe themselves to be, leaving behind digital footprints. People who cyberbully through text messaging may also be traced by their phone numbers.**

**Internet service providers (such as Verizon or AT&T) and social-networking sites (like Facebook) can also trace messages. If a person sends an email message or posts a comment on a**

Duplicating this page is illegal. Do not copy this material without written permission from the publisher.

**social-networking site, the message can often be traced to the person or computer—even if he or she used a different screen name or sent something anonymously.**

**If people keep copies of the bullying messages they've received and are able to trace who sent them, the sender may end up in trouble with the law.**

**This happened to a sixteen-year-old boy in Georgia who used a screen name to send threatening messages and write threats on a social-networking site. Some students contacted the school and the police were called in. The student was identified and arrested after an investigation showed who he was.**

2. Read and discuss your school's policy regarding cyberbullying, if available.

3. Use a Smart Board or whiteboard and write the following headings:

   A person who cyberbullies…          A person who doesn't cyberbully…

4. Ask:

   **How do you think a person might feel about himself or herself and others if he or she chooses to cyberbully or join in cyberbullying others?**

   Allow several students to answer this question. Write their answers in the left-hand column.

   Possible answers include that the person doesn't care about others, is jealous of others, always wants to get even, likes to tease people in mean ways, likes to hurt people's feelings, and likes to feel powerful.

Duplicating this page is illegal. Do not copy this material without written permission from the publisher.

**How do you think other students might feel about a classmate who engages in cyberbullying?** (Emphasize that most don't like it.)

5. Then in the right-hand column, generate a list of how a person who chooses not to cyberbully might feel about himself or herself and others.

   Possible answers include that the person knows how to empathize with others, is considerate of others, knows how to make friends, knows how to keep friends, knows how to interact well with others, knows how to deal with feelings, knows how to have fun, takes responsibility for his or her actions, knows how to make good decisions, and is someone people can trust.

6. Summarize by saying:

   **If you are involved in cyberbullying or see it when you are online, think about the choices you want to make and how you want to treat others before you decide to join in. When you decide not to join in, think about whether there's anything you could do to stop it.**

Duplicating this page is illegal. Do not copy this material without written permission from the publisher.

89

**PART 2**

20 minutes

▶ **Stop Cyberbullying**

The purpose of part 2 is for students to take a stand against cyberbullying in their school. The peer-led groups will be creating a public service announcement, or PSA. A PSA is a noncommercial advertisement usually made to raise awareness about an issue or cause.

The PSAs that students will create can take the form of a poster, an announcement over your school's public-address system, or a video shown on your school's closed-circuit TV system. If you are limited on time, having all students work on creating posters would be best.

Whatever format students decide to use, it is important that their PSAs be heard or seen, so students realize they are taking actual steps to stop or prevent cyberbullying. Depending on what medium your students use, you may need to include extra class time or have students continue their work in another class, such as an art or media class.

You might also assign portions of this project as a homework assignment. Another option would be to have students present their PSAs to each other when they present their final project to the whole class in session 8. You could also encourage students to hang their posters around the school, show their video PSAs over your closed-circuit TV system (if available), and read them over the PA system during morning or afternoon announcements.

1. Explain to the students:

   **Now that you know a lot about what cyberbullying is, how it affects people, and why people might think they can get away with it, it's time to start doing something about it. How many of you know what a public service announcement is?**

   **A public service announcement, also called a PSA, is an advertisement that's not selling something. It's usually designed to get people thinking about an issue or cause.**

Duplicating this page is illegal. Do not copy this material without written permission from the publisher.

In your small groups, you will create public service announcements about preventing or stopping cyberbullying.

**TEACHER TIP**
*Prior to class, do an Internet search for PSAs about cyberbullying to see some examples.*

You may have seen or heard similar announcements about smoking or drug prevention. They usually have a message and a clever or eye-catching way of getting that message across. Can you think of some PSAs that you have seen or heard recently on television or on the radio? Have you seen any in newspapers and magazines?

2. Explain:

Each small group will use a planning sheet to plan your PSA. Then you will have an opportunity to create a PSA that you will present to other students at our school.

S4-3

3. Give each peer leader a PSA Planning Sheet. Briefly go through the sheet by explaining:

The target audience is the group of people your PSA is intended to reach. Maybe you will want to make one that is aimed at girls your age or maybe you want to target boys and girls younger than you. It's up to your group to decide.

Decide what your message will be. You should be able to state this in one sentence, for example, "Most students at Central Middle School don't cyberbully and don't like it when they see it."

**TEACHER TIP**
*If students do not have a choice of the medium they can use, simply tell them what kind of PSA they will be creating.*

Decide what medium you will use. Your choices are posters, videos, or audio, such as a PSA that could be heard on the radio or on our school's PA system.

Explain equipment use or availability if groups are doing audio or video projects.

Duplicating this page is illegal. Do not copy this material without written permission from the publisher.

**Describing the PSA means that you will outline or plan it. You should write a detailed description so it will be easy to create it from that description. For example, if you are making a poster, your description will explain what it looks like and what words will be on it. If you are creating a PSA for the radio, you will write the dialogue and who is speaking, just like a play script. If you are making a video, you will write what is happening in the scene, where it is taking place, what is being said, and who is saying it.**

**Decide who will do each part of the PSA. For example, who will be the printer, artist, actor, speaker, or cameraperson.**

4. Tell each group that they will need to fill out the planning sheet and show it to you before they move to the next step of making the PSA.

5. Allow time for students to work on their PSAs, or assign portions of this work as a homework assignment.

6. If possible, have students show or present their PSAs to the rest of the class or to the school when they are finished, or during session 8.

Duplicating this page is illegal. Do not copy this material without written permission from the publisher.

**PART 3**
5 minutes

▶ **Conclusion and Homework Assignment**

1. Explain:

   **Congratulations on taking steps to prevent cyberbullying in our school! You can also prevent cyberbullying by what you do (or don't do) when you see cyberbullying happening. For example, the next time you see a text message that you know is cyberbullying, take a stand.**

   **You can take a stand by not responding to the message or by not forwarding it to others. You can also take a stand by sending a message back telling the sender that cyberbullying is not okay or by reporting it to an adult. We will learn more about taking a stand during our next session.**

2. Tell the students where their posters will be posted or when their PSAs will be heard or shown to the rest of the school or at least another class. Explore posting some at another school, a local library, mall, or other community setting to help raise awareness about cyberbullying.

   S4-4 (SP)

3. Hand out Homework Assignment 4 to each student. Explain to the students:

   **This is a homework assignment for you to do with a parent or another adult you live with. If it is not possible for an adult you live with to do it with you, then another adult, such as a relative or neighbor, could do it with you. If you have trouble finding an adult to do it with you, come and see me, and I will help you. These are the activities this week:**

   • **The adult has some information to read.**

   • **You both make family rules about technology use.**

Duplicating this page is illegal. Do not copy this material without written permission from the publisher.

**When you and the adult you are working with have completed the homework assignment, both of you need to sign the return slip at the bottom of the sheet and you need to bring that part back to class.**

If you are posting the journal entries online, have students read through today's entries again and answer this question online:

> What is the difference between saying something mean to someone's face and using technology to send something mean to someone?

If you are posting the real-life stories online, have students read through today's story again and answer these questions online:

> If you were to come across a website like the one Yvette created about Lucy, what would your reaction be? What could you do about it?

4. Show the students where to put their homework slips.

5. Explain how students will be graded on this homework assignment.

6. Tell the students when the homework assignment will be due.

Duplicating this page is illegal. Do not copy this material without written permission from the publisher.

## CYBERBULLYING

SESSION 5

# How Should You React to Cyberbullying?

## Description

Through journal entries or a real-life story, small- and large-group discussions, and sample situations, students will learn what to do if someone cyberbullies them or another person.

## Learner Outcomes

By the end of this session, students will be able to

- identify what steps to take if they are cyberbullied.

- identify what steps to take if they know someone else is being cyberbullied.

## Materials Needed

☐ CD-ROM materials:

 **Grade 6–8**
- Session 5 Journal Entries  S5-1

 **Grade 9–12**
- Session 5 Real-Life Story ▢ S5-2

- Do First poster and handout ▢ I-15, S5-3

- Question Cube Template ▢ S5-4

- What Would You Do If...? situation sheets ▢ S5-5

- Homework Assignment 5 ▢ S5-6 (SP)

---

### SESSION 5 AT A GLANCE

**Total Time: 50 minutes**

*Part 1:*
Journal Entries/
Real-Life Story
and Discussion
*(25 minutes)*

*Part 2:*
Practice Saying "No"
to Cyberbullying
*(20 minutes)*

*Part 3:*
Conclusion
and Homework
Assignment
*(5 minutes)*

Duplicating this page is illegal. Do not copy this material without written permission from the publisher.

☐ Smart Board or whiteboard

☐ Your school's bullying/cyberbullying policy, if available

☐ Scissors

☐ Clear tape

## Preparation Needed

1. Print out the Session 5 Journal Entries, one set per student.

   Students will be working on the journal entries in their small groups. Each small group will work on a different character and all students in that small group will need a copy of that character's journal entry. However, you may wish to give all students a copy of all four journal entries to follow along as they are read aloud. You may also want to have extra copies so that members of a small group could discuss a second character if they finish their work early.

2. Print out the Session 5 Real-Life Story, one copy per student.

3. Print out the Do First poster; enlarge and display it in your space.

4. Print out the Do First handout, one copy per student.

5. Print out the Question Cube Template, one per small group. Cut out and assemble the cubes. (This could also be done by the peer leaders.)

6. Print out the What Would You Do If...? situation sheets, one set per small group. Select the situation for your classroom, cut them out, and have them ready for each peer leader.

7. Print out Homework Assignment 5, one copy per student.

Duplicating this page is illegal. Do not copy this material without written permission from the publisher.

**SESSION 5 OUTLINE**

**PART 1**
25 minutes

▶ **Journal Entries/Real-Life Story and Discussion**

The purpose of part 1 is to identify the steps to take if you or someone you know is being cyberbullied.

 S5-1  Grade 6–8 **Journal Entries**

1. Explain to the students:

   **During the last session, we talked about why people think they can get away with cyberbullying. What are some of the reasons?**

   Allow time for students to respond.

**TEACHER TIP**
*An alternative to paper and pencil journal entries would be to post the journal entries on a blog or message board accessible only to you and your students. This will help extend the learning. Suggestions for online homework related to the journal entries are included at the end of this session.*

   **You also did a good job of making PSAs so students in our school and people in our community are more aware of cyberbullying. Since we know that it does happen, today we will talk about what to do if cyberbullying happens to you, someone you know, or even someone you don't know. And we'll read more about Allie, J.T., Serena, and Aaron to see what happens.**

2. Hand out the Session 5 Journal Entries to the class. Read the journal entries or have students read them aloud as the rest of the class follows along.

3. After the journal entries have been read, divide the class into the same peer-led small groups and have them go to their designated areas in the classroom.

4. Assign one character in the journal entries to each small group, making sure each group has a different character than

Duplicating this page is illegal. Do not copy this material without written permission from the publisher.

**TEACHER TIP**
*If one group finishes its discussion before the others, those students could work on the discussion questions of a second character.*

**TEACHER TIP**
*As students report back about their discussions, you may need to guide or reframe their answers to correct misconceptions as they arise.*

 S5-2 | Grade 6–8

the one it worked on last time. If there are more than four small groups, two groups can work on the journal entry of the same character. Have each small group discuss the questions related to its assigned character.

5. Allow 7 to 10 minutes for small groups to discuss the questions for the characters they are assigned.

6. When the groups are ready, call on the peer leaders to read aloud to the class their groups' answers to the questions. Call on all of the groups with the same character together.

## Real-Life Story

1. Explain to the students:

   **During the last session, we talked about why people think they can get away with cyberbullying. What are some of the reasons?**

   Allow time for students to respond.

   **You also did a good job of making PSAs so students in our school and people in our community are more aware of cyberbullying. Since we know that cyberbullying does happen, today we will talk about what to do if cyberbullying happens to you, someone you know, or even someone you don't know. And we'll be reading another real-life story that will help us learn more.**

**TEACHER TIP**
*An alternative to paper and pencil real-life stories would be to post these on a blog or message board accessible only to you and your students. This will help extend the learning. Suggestions for online homework related to the story are included at the end of this session.*

2. Hand out the Session 5 Real-Life Story to the class. At the beginning of the story is a paragraph describing the incident. Read the paragraph aloud. Then choose students or ask for volunteers to read the other sections of the story aloud.

3. After the real-life story has been read, divide the class into the same peer-led small groups and have them go to their designated areas in the classroom.

Duplicating this page is illegal. Do not copy this material without written permission from the publisher.

4. Allow 7 to 10 minutes for the small groups to discuss the questions related to the story.

5. When the groups are ready, call the class back to order. Assign each group a question to answer first in front of the group to spark discussion. (If there are more groups than questions, double-up groups on a question and allow all of them to read their responses before discussion.) After the designated group has given its answers, invite other groups to respond and give their answers. Some answers may be repeated, but this format allows thoughtful discussion.

### Discussion Summary: Do First

1. Write these two headings on a whiteboard or Smart Board:

   If you were cyberbullied...      If someone else were
                                    cyberbullied...

**TEACHER TIP**
*Depending on students' answers, you may need to comment or gently guide students to more appropriate and safer solutions.*

2. After students report back on their small-group discussions, ask them about what they could do if they or someone else they know were cyberbullied. List their ideas of what to do under each heading.

3. Summarize their answers by saying:

   **You've already come up with some good ideas about what to do if you or someone you know is being cyberbullied. If it happens to you or a friend, or someone you know even if they're not your good friend, you will probably find it upsetting and wonder what you should do first. Here is a list to help you remember what to do or how to help someone else.**

   **You can remember this list using the acronym Do First. Each letter in these two words represents a step you can take to address cyberbullying. As a friend of someone who is being**

Duplicating this page is illegal. Do not copy this material without written permission from the publisher.

99

cyberbullied, you could help that person remember these steps as well.

I-15
S5-3

4. Display the Do First poster. Distribute a copy of the Do First handout to each student. Discuss the points on the poster using the language provided:

*D*o not retaliate. **When people find out that something mean or nasty or untrue is being said about them, they often want to get back at whoever did it. Not only will that make things worse, but you will be giving the person who is cyberbullying what he or she wants—a reaction from you.**

**The people who are cyberbullying may think they have power over you because you can't see them, but they also can't see your reaction. Sometimes people bully others to make them mad and upset, so don't let them have their way. If you don't try to get back at them, they might think it didn't matter to you and may leave you alone. But, if you do try to get back at them, the students who are cyberbullying could use what you did as evidence against you instead.**

*O*ff your friends or followers list! **If you've been bullied through texting or a social-networking site such as Facebook or Twitter, remove the profile name from your list so the person won't bother you any more. It's possible that they may start to bully you with another user name or in another way, however, so be on the lookout.**

*F*igure out who it is. **If you've been bullied through text messages on your cell phone, you can trace and block the number through your phone. If you know who it is, you might decide to avoid that person if it's someone at school. Or you might think of a possible response, which is different from retaliation. We'll talk more about this in a few minutes.**

Duplicating this page is illegal. Do not copy this material without written permission from the publisher.

If you are receiving threatening email messages, these can be reported to your Internet service provider. You can get an adult to help you with this. Most social-networking sites also have ways to report abuse online, such as Facebook's social reporting tools. If you are receiving messages or posts that threaten your safety or someone else's safety, you need to talk to an adult right away.

*I*gnore it. Sometimes just ignoring it makes the people who are cyberbullying stop, because their actions are not having the effect they're hoping for. If someone sends only one mean email, you can probably ignore it.

*R*espond after you think about it carefully. A response is different than retaliation. You might be hurt or angry or upset, but you don't want to give the people who are cyberbullying the satisfaction of knowing it. So if you choose to respond, make it clear and cool. Don't give the people who are bullying anything that could be used as bullying evidence against you.

*S*ave the evidence! This is very important! Save anything that is harmful—even the messages you decide to ignore— in case more of them come later. If the bullying continues, you will need to have evidence before steps can be taken to make it stop. You can save evidence by printing it, copying and saving it, or just not erasing it. But, once you do this, you may want to delete the online comments so that you or others don't continue to see them.

*T*ell an adult! If you receive or are aware of threatening or disturbing messages, it is important that you tell an adult immediately. This could be an adult at school or an adult at home. Here at our school, we will take all reports of cyberbullying very seriously. Let's talk about whom you might tell at our school.

Duplicating this page is illegal. Do not copy this material without written permission from the publisher.

Have a brief discussion that makes clear that students can tell you or any adult at school, but highlight any specific procedures your school has in place to report cyberbullying or bullying of any kind. You may also want to revisit your school's policy, if available.

**There have been serious situations at some schools that might have been prevented if students had told someone about disturbing and threatening messages that they were aware of.**

5. Remind students:

**If you have a friend who is being cyberbullied, he or she will need your support. The person might also need your help deciding what to do. If you are encouraged to join in cyberbullying, or if someone sends you emails or messages about someone else, respond by saying that you think it's mean and you won't send it to anyone else. Because adults don't always know when cyberbullying is going on, you may need to tell them and ask them to help stop it.**

Duplicating this page is illegal. Do not copy this material without written permission from the publisher.

**PART 2**
20 minutes

▶ **Practice Saying "No" to Cyberbullying**

The purpose of part 2 is to give students the opportunity to practice how they would react to cyberbullying situations if they were cyberbullied, the friend of someone who was cyberbullied, or a bystander aware of a cyberbullying situation.

1. Explain to the students:

   **You will now have a chance to practice using the Do First steps to figure out how to help someone who is being cyberbullied.**

S5-4

**TEACHER TIP**
*You may want to choose which situations you would like your class to discuss, depending on the age of your students and their experiences with cyberbullying in your community. To do this, copy only the situations you want to use and make your own What Would You Do If...? situation sheet.*

   - **Each small group will receive a Question Cube with questions on it.**

   - **Each group's peer leader will read a situation, and you will take turns rolling the cube gently and answering the question that is on top.**

   - **These questions are on the cube:**

     - **What would you do if this happened to you?**

     - **What would you do if this happened to a friend?**

     - **What would you do if you heard about it or saw it?**

     - **What would you do if you knew who did the bullying?**

     - **What would you do if this happened to someone you didn't like?** (This should not change how someone would act.)

     - **The cube includes a special situation question. This question is at the end of the situation on the sheet and is only about that particular situation.**

   - **Two people might get the same question. Since they might do something different, they could answer the same question. If a question has been answered twice, the next**

Duplicating this page is illegal. Do not copy this material without written permission from the publisher.

104

student to get that question should roll the cube again for a new question.

• After everyone in the group has had a turn, the peer leader will read the next situation.

S5-5   2. Hand out the What Would You Do If…? situations to each peer leader.

3. Allow students 10 to 15 minutes for small groups to use the Question Cube to discuss their situations.

4. Circulate among the groups to monitor their discussions.

Duplicating this page is illegal. Do not copy this material without written permission from the publisher.

**PART 3**
5 minutes

▶ **Conclusion and Homework Assignment**

1. Ask:

   **Which situations do you think might happen in this school? Were any of these situations similar to ones that you already know about?**

   Allow time for discussion between questions.

2. Remind students about the Do First handout and tell them to keep this in a special place so they can refer to it as needed.

 S5-6 (SP)

3. Hand out Homework Assignment 5. Explain to the students:

   **This is a homework assignment for you to do with a parent or an adult you live with. If it is not possible for an adult you live with to do the assignment with you, then another adult, such as a relative or neighbor, could do it with you. If you have trouble finding an adult to do it with you, come and see me, and I will help you. These are the activities this week:**

   • **The adult has some information to read.**

   • **You both make commitments to stop or prevent cyberbullying.**

   **When you and the adult you are working with have completed the homework assignment, both of you need to sign the return slip at the bottom of the last page and you need to bring that part back to class.**

Grade
6–8

   If you are posting the journal entries online, have students read through today's entries again and tell them to do the following assignment online. If you are not posting the journal entries online, students will need to complete this assignment on paper and turn it in.

Duplicating this page is illegal. Do not copy this material without written permission from the publisher.

**TEACHER TIP**

*If time permits, you can briefly discuss these homework assignment paragraphs at the beginning of session 6. However, they should also be handed in for grading and feedback from you.*

**One of your homework assignments for this session will be to choose one of the two situations talked about in the journal entries—Aaron and the cyberbullying of his teacher or the situation with Allie, J.T., and Serena. Using what you've learned, especially the Do First steps, write a paragraph that explains how you would work out the situation in a positive and respectful way. This paragraph will be due at the next session on _____** *(insert date).*

If you are posting the real-life stories online, have students do the following assignment online. If you are not posting the real-life stories online, students will need to complete this assignment on paper and turn it in.

**One of your homework assignments for this session will be to search online or in the newspaper for a story about cyberbullying. Using what you've learned, especially the Do First steps, write a paragraph that explains how you would resolve the situation in a positive and respectful way. This paragraph will be due at the next session on _____** *(insert date).*

4. Show the students where to put their homework slips.

5. Explain how students will be graded on this homework assignment.

6. Tell the students when the homework will be due.

Duplicating this page is illegal. Do not copy this material without written permission from the publisher.

# Creating a Positive Social-Networking Site or App, Part I

## Description

Through a small-group project, students will create plans for their own social-networking sites or apps that will promote safe and positive Internet use.

## Learner Outcomes

By the end of this session, students will be able to

- describe how some social-networking sites began.

- explain what social-networking sites do to curb abuse.

- describe the steps in planning a social-networking site or app.

- describe rules for belonging to some social-networking sites.

The small-group project of creating a plan for a social-networking site or app will be introduced in this session. Students will work in their peer-led small groups. The students will continue to work on this project during session 7. Each small group will give a 5-minute class presentation about its site or app during session 8. You may wish to give more class time to this project or assign some of the project work as homework.

**SESSION 6 AT A GLANCE**

Total Time: 50 minutes

*Part 1:*
Introduction
*(15 minutes)*

*Part 2:*
Getting Started
*(30 minutes)*

*Part 3:*
Conclusion
*(5 minutes)*

Duplicating this page is illegal. Do not copy this material without written permission from the publisher.

## Materials Needed

☐ CD-ROM materials:

- Facebook Statement of Rights and Responsibilities ▯ **S6-2**

- Social-Networking Site or App Planning Packet ▯ **S6-3**

- Facts of the Feature sheet ▯ **S6-4**

- Session 6 Journal Entries ▯ **S6-1**

☐ Smart Board or whiteboard

**Grade 6–8**

## Preparation Needed

1. Show the Facebook information using a Smart Board or write it on a whiteboard.

2. Print out the Social-Networking Site or App Planning Packet, one copy per small group.

3. Print out the Facts of the Feature sheet, one or two copies per student.

4. Make copies of the Session 6 Journal Entries, one set per student.

**Grade 6–8**

5. Visit some social-networking sites so you are familiar with their format and content.

Duplicating this page is illegal. Do not copy this material without written permission from the publisher.

**PART 1**
15 minutes

**TEACHER TIP**
*The written paragraphs from session 5 are due at this time. Collect or print them to read and comment on and/or have students read their paragraphs aloud, if time permits.*

▶ **Introduction**

The purpose of part 1 is to introduce the small-group project in which students will create a plan for a social-networking site or app that promotes positive and safe Internet use.

1. Explain to the students:

**Today we will talk about social-networking sites. What are some examples of social-networking sites you know of?**

Possible answers include Twitter, Facebook, Instagram, Snapchat, and Ask.fm.

2. Ask:

**Why do you think we should talk about these sites in a program about cyberbullying?**

One possible answer is because a lot of cyberbullying goes on through these sites.

**What are some examples of cyberbullying or inappropriate use of social-networking sites that you have seen or heard about?**

Caution students to not use names or too many details.

**What are some examples of positive ways to use these sites? What do you like about them?**

Allow time between questions for students to answer.

**What if you could create your own positive social-networking site or app? What kinds of features would you like to have on it? What would it look like?**

Duplicating this page is illegal. Do not copy this material without written permission from the publisher.

Allow time between questions for students to answer.

3. Summarize by saying:

**You have a lot of good ideas. And actually that's how these sites started—a few people who knew computers had a lot of good ideas.**

**The following are examples of how certain sites began. Guess which sites they are.**

Example 1:

**Three guys who took digital photos and videos at a party wanted to figure out how they could download them and send them to their friends so they could see them without having a special software program. When they figured it out, what site did they create?**

The answer is YouTube.

Example 2:

**A man named Tom Anderson and some computer programmers set up this site in 2003. It allows people to share information about themselves. The site and the company that owned it were bought for 580 million dollars in 2005.**

The answer is MySpace.

Example 3:

**A college student started this site as a hobby and as a way for college students to share information about themselves. It spread to other colleges and eventually became what site?**

The answer is Facebook.

Example 4:

**What site began as a short messaging service (SMS) for a podcasting company?**

Duplicating this page is illegal. Do not copy this material without written permission from the publisher.

The answer is Twitter.

Example 5:

**This site was created in 2005 to be an online world where children could play games, have fun, and interact. Two years later it became part of the Disney family.**

The answer is Club Penguin.

Example 6:

**What website was started by a company that makes stuffed animals?**

The answer is Webkinz.

4. Ask:

**How do these sites make money if you don't pay for them?**

A possible answer is advertising. Also, companies want as many people as possible to see their advertisements, and they pay a lot of money to have them on sites that are very popular with an age group that has a lot of money—for example, tweens and teens!

**TEACHER TIP**

*Tweens are nine- to thirteen-year-olds.*

5. Ask:

**Are there age limits for these sites?**

The answer is yes; most require users to be at least 13, but this can be difficult to enforce.

6. Ask:

**What about cyberbullying? Do you know what these sites do, if anything, to prevent cyberbullying or inappropriate use of the site?**

Duplicating this page is illegal. Do not copy this material without written permission from the publisher.

Possible answers include these:

- All sites have terms of use.

- It is possible to report misuse and abuse of these sites if the behavior is against their rules.

- They will also remove underage user profiles.

7. Display the Facebook Statement of Rights and Responsibilities on a Smart Board.

S6-2

8. Explain to the students:

**This is the Statement of Rights and Responsibilities from Facebook. Its website also has links to report misuse or abuse.**

9. Briefly go through the Facebook statement.

10. Summarize by saying:

**One of the features that the people who created these sites had to consider is how to keep these sites safe, which works sometimes, but not all the time.**

11. Explain to the students:

**The people who started these social-networking sites had three main things—ideas, ingenuity, and investors. The ideas were theirs, they were smart and clever enough to develop them, and then they got some big money from investors who saw a way to make even more money through these sites.**

**Today we are going to imagine that a company called TechyTeen is interested in investing millions of dollars in a new social-networking site or app that encourages safe and positive interactions among tweens and teens.**

Duplicating this page is illegal. Do not copy this material without written permission from the publisher.

You will be working in your small groups using your ideas and ingenuity—those are your brains and creativity—to come up with a plan for a site or app like this. You will have today and _____ *(insert date of next session)* to work on this. Then you will present your plan to the rest of the class. The site or app can have many different features and capabilities—it's up to you. Here is the information from the TechyTeen Company:

12. Read the following fictional notice aloud to the whole class:

We at the TechyTeen Company are interested in investing a minimum of 25 million dollars to start up a new social-networking site or app for tweens and teens. We envision the site or app to have several different features that promote positive interactions between tweens and teens and the world around them. We see this site or app as being safe and secure for all users. We are open to new ideas and suggestions. Please do not restrict your proposals in any way due to cost. Here are our main guidelines in judging these proposals:

- by how strongly they appeal to tweens and teens

- by how safe they are

- by how well they promote positive interactions among teens and their world

Thank you very much for your interest,
          The TechyTeen Company

13. Briefly discuss the following questions to get students thinking about the site/app project:

What are some ways that a site or app could be appealing to both tweens *and* teens?

Duplicating this page is illegal. Do not copy this material without written permission from the publisher.

Possible answers include the layout, topics, and features.

**What are some ways a site or app could be made safe?**

Possible answers include that people have to sign a form saying they won't do certain things, people have to register with their real contact information to be able to use the site, people have a way to report cyberbullying or illegal behavior, information about cyberbullying is provided on the site, and the site automatically makes profiles private for users under the age of eighteen.

**What are some ways that a site or app could promote positive interactions among teens and their world?**

Possible answers include features that look for the best instead of the worst, compliment boards, writing stories about positive things people are doing in the world, and creating positive campaigns that raise money for good causes.

14. Divide the class into the peer-led small groups.

15. Explain that the role of the peer leader in these groups is to keep the group on task and to make sure everyone plays a role in getting the project done.

S6-3
S6-4
16. Hand out a Social-Networking Site or App Planning Packet to each small group. Also distribute Facts of the Feature sheets to each student.

17. Briefly go through the packet, emphasizing these points:

   • **On the first day** (*or* **today), you will decide the name of your site or app and what features will be on it. These could be movie reviews, photo sharing, comment pages, profiles, and so on.**

Duplicating this page is illegal. Do not copy this material without written permission from the publisher.

- As a group you will brainstorm what these features will be. Then each of you will choose at least one feature to describe in detail using the Facts of the Feature sheet.

- You might need to take more time at home to finish these steps.

- During the next session on _____ *(insert date),* you will read your Facts of the Feature sheets to each other, discuss them, and talk about the look and layout of the features and the site or app. After that, you will draw the layout of the features and the site's or app's home page.

- You will come up with a policy, or rules, that will keep the site or app safe and free from cyberbullying.

- At the end of the next session, you will decide who will do each part of your class presentation of your social-networking site or app plan on _____ *(insert date).* The presentations should be no more than 5 minutes long.

- Remember you are trying to impress the TechyTeen Company so it gives your group 25 million dollars to set up this site or app. Keep in mind the three things that are most important to the company—appealing to tweens and teens, safety for users, and positive interactions among tweens and teens throughout the world.

Duplicating this page is illegal. Do not copy this material without written permission from the publisher.

**PART 2**
30 minutes

▶ **Getting Started**

The purpose of part 2 is for students to work on their social-networking site or app projects.

1. Allow time for students to work on their projects.

2. Circulate among the groups to make sure they are on task and understand the assignment.

Duplicating this page is illegal. Do not copy this material without written permission from the publisher.

**PART 3**
5 minutes

▶ **Conclusion**

1. Remind students that they need to have the Facts of the Feature sheets filled out for the next session on _____ *(insert date)*.

2. Summarize the session by saying that this is their chance to be web designers and for them to show their creativity in making a plan for a positive website or app for tweens and teens.

**Journal Entries**

3. Explain:

**I will be reading through your conclusions for the journal entries. But I thought you might want to know how things turned out for Allie, J.T., Serena, and Aaron. Your only homework for this session is to read these journal entries so you know what happened.**

 S6-1

Hand out the Session 6 Journal Entries.

There is no take-home parent-student activity for this session.

Duplicating this page is illegal. Do not copy this material without written permission from the publisher.

117

# Creating a Positive Social-Networking Site or App, Part II

## Description

Students will fill out a form to commit to helping stop cyberbullying and to explain what they will do if they are aware of cyberbullying situations. Students will also continue to work on their website/app project plans.

## Learner Outcomes

By the end of this session, students will be able to

- describe the components of an effective presentation.

- identify how they personally will commit themselves to stop or prevent cyberbullying.

## Materials Needed

- ☐ CD-ROM materials:
  - Social-Networking Site or App Planning Packet from session 6
  - Cyber Solutions sheet S7-1

- ☐ Materials for the project, including large paper or poster board, markers, and colored pencils

- ☐ *Optional:* Computers

---

**SESSION 7 AT A GLANCE**

**Total Time: 50 minutes**

*Part 1:*
Introduction
(5 minutes)

*Part 2:*
Creating a Positive Social-Networking Site or App, Part II
(40 minutes)

*Part 3:*
Conclusion
(5 minutes)

Duplicating this page is illegal. Do not copy this material without written permission from the publisher.

119

**Preparation Needed**

1. Print out the Cyber Solutions sheet, one copy per student.

2. Gather project materials.

Duplicating this page is illegal. Do not copy this material without written permission from the publisher.

**PART 1**
5 minutes

▶ **Introduction**

The purpose of part 1 is for students to think about their commitment to stop and/or prevent cyberbullying.

1. Explain to the students:

   **We are almost at the end of our unit on cyberbullying, but this won't be the end of our discussions about cyberbullying. In fact, this should just be the beginning of your promise to prevent cyberbullying and help others who are being cyberbullied. I am going to hand out a Cyber Solutions sheet to each of you. You will need to complete the sheet for the next session on _____ *(insert date)* when you will be giving your presentations.**

S7-1

2. Hand out the Cyber Solutions sheet now. As time permits, you could allow class time for students to complete the form before the next session.

Duplicating this page is illegal. Do not copy this material without written permission from the publisher.

**PART 2**
40 minutes

▶ **Creating a Positive Social-Networking Site or App, Part II**

The purpose of part 2 is for the students to continue to work on the small-group project.

1. Explain to the students that they will now have time to work on their social-networking site project.

2. Remind students:

   **You should have completed your Facts of the Feature sheets by now. Today you will go over these features in your small groups. Then you will design the layout for these features, as well as the home page for the website or app. You will also need to decide what safety features and policies will be included. By the end of the session, you will also choose who will do each part of your team's presentation on**

   _____ *(insert date)*.

3. Remind students that the TechyTeen Company is willing to spend 25 million dollars on a social-networking site or app that is appealing to tweens and teens, is safe, and promotes positive interactions among teens around the world.

4. Hand out materials, including large pieces of paper, poster boards, markers, and colored pencils, for students to use in their website or app designs. Point out the pages in the Social-Networking Site or App Planning Packet (Day 2) for recording the group's plans.

   *Optional:* If you have the resources, invite the groups to create their website or app plans on the computer in a PowerPoint presentation.

5. Allow the rest of the class period for students to work on their projects.

Duplicating this page is illegal. Do not copy this material without written permission from the publisher.

**PART 3**
5 minutes

▶ **Conclusion**

1. Remind students to finish up any work that they have not completed in time for their project presentations on _____ *(insert date)*.

2. Remind students to be thoughtful when they fill out the Cyber Solutions sheet and make a commitment to help stop cyberbullying. Let them know that they will be sharing one of their commitments with the class during the next session.

   There is no take-home parent-student activity for this session.

Duplicating this page is illegal. Do not copy this material without written permission from the publisher.

# Creating a Positive Social-Networking Site or App, Part III

## Description

Students will read one of their commitments to the class about how they will stop and/or prevent cyberbullying. They will also present their social-networking site/app project plans to the class. If students have not already done so and if time permits, have them share their PSAs from session 4.

## Learner Outcomes

By the end of this session, students will be able to

- make a public commitment to prevent cyberbullying.

- identify positive ways to use social-networking sites.

## Materials Needed

☐ CD-ROM materials:

- Social-Networking Site or App Plan Presentation Score Sheet ▢ S8-1

☐ *Optional:* Video camera to film the presentations

**SESSION 8
AT A GLANCE**

Total Time: 50 minutes

*Part 1:*
Introduction
*(10 minutes)*

*Part 2:*
Presenting Your
Positive Social-
Networking Sites
or Apps
*(35 minutes)*

*Part 3:*
Conclusion
*(5 minutes)*

Duplicating this page is illegal. Do not copy this material without written permission from the publisher.

## Preparation Needed

1. Print the Social-Networking Site or App Plan Presentation Score Sheet, one copy per student.

2. *Optional:* Make sure the video camera is ready for filming.

3. Mark your calendar for one or two months from today. Set aside some time on that day to give the Cyber Solutions sheets back to the students to look at them again. Have a brief discussion at that time about whether students have acted or have had to act on these commitments. (Caution them not to share names or identifying details in a group setting.)

4. If possible, invite a school administrator to listen to your students' presentations. This person could act as a representative for the TechyTeen Company and pretend to award the 25 million dollars to one group. Or each group could be given an award based on criteria such as these:

   - most appealing to teens

   - safest website or app

   - best at promoting the most positive interactions among teens around the world

   - most creative

   - most organized

   - most original

   - best presentation

   - most user-friendly

Duplicating this page is illegal. Do not copy this material without written permission from the publisher.

S E S S I O N  O U T L I N E

**PART 1**
10 minutes

▶ **Introduction**

1. Tell students to take out their Cyber Solutions sheets. They should have these filled out and signed.

2. Go around the room and ask each student to read one of his or her statements aloud to the class so everyone will have heard one commitment from everyone else.

3. Congratulate the students for committing themselves to help prevent cyberbullying.

4. Collect the Cyber Solutions sheets from the students.

5. Explain:

   **You will look at these sheets again later in the year to discuss whether and how you have acted on these promises.**

Duplicating this page is illegal. Do not copy this material without written permission from the publisher.

127

**PART 2**

35 minutes

▶ **Presenting Your Positive Social-Networking Sites or Apps**

The purpose of part 2 is to have students present their social-networking site/app project plans.

Depending on the number of small groups in your class, student presentations may take another class period to complete.

1. Explain:

   **I will call each group to the front to present your project plan to the class. Remember that 25 million dollars is at stake for the best proposal.**

 S8-1

2. Give each student a Social-Networking Site or App Plan Presentation Score Sheet. Tell the students to fill this out as each group gives its presentation. They will score each group (except their own) based on how well the group addressed TechyTeen's criteria of appeal to teens, safety, and positive interactions among teens around the world. The scores will range from 1 to 5 with 1 being the lowest and 5 being the highest. The students will also write on their score sheets one thing they liked about each website/app plan.

3. Remind students that this is not a popularity contest and that you will be grading their score sheets to make sure they were paying attention.

4. Call on each group to give its presentation.

5. Remind the students to speak slowly and loudly so everyone can hear them.

6. Allow a moment for questions or comments after each presentation.

Duplicating this page is illegal. Do not copy this material without written permission from the publisher.

7. After all of the presentations have been given, collect the Social-Networking Site or App Plan Presentation Score Sheets from students.

8. *Option A:* Tally the score sheets for each group and announce a winner at a later date.

   *Option B:* Reward the (fake) 25 million dollar check to the group that you (or the school administrator attending) think gave the best presentation.

   *Option C:* Hand out a unique award to each group. Ideas for these unique awards were suggested in this session's Preparation Needed section on page 126.

   *Option D:* Tell the class that each presentation had something that could be used on the new website or in an app, so the entire class could work together and win the 25 million dollars.

Duplicating this page is illegal. Do not copy this material without written permission from the publisher.

**PART 3**
5 minutes

▶ **Conclusion**

1. Congratulate the students on their presentations.

2. Summarize by saying:

> You have learned a lot about cyberbullying in the past few weeks. You know how harmful it can be and how to deal with it if it happens to you or someone you know. We'll continue to talk about cyberbullying every once in a while in our class meetings *(or "in class" if class meetings aren't held)*. I hope you'll take seriously the need to stop cyberbullying and all forms of bullying.
>
> Stopping cyberbullying begins with everyone making a commitment not to do it, not to spread it or join in, and to report it when it happens. You can begin by using social-networking sites and other kinds of technology in a positive way. What you do can make a big difference!

Duplicating this page is illegal. Do not copy this material without written permission from the publisher.

## ADDITIONAL **MATERIALS**

## Teacher Training Preparation

### Description

This outline includes directions for conducting a 3-hour training for facilitators and teachers of *Cyberbullying: A Prevention Curriculum for Grades 6–12*. Adapt this outline to fit the needs and timeframe of your group.

### Who Should Conduct the Training?

Ideally, several staff and faculty members at the school who help to coordinate the school's bullying prevention activities will conduct the training. For schools that are implementing the *Olweus Bullying Prevention Program (OBPP)*, this training would be led by individuals on the Bullying Prevention Coordinating Committee. If such a committee does not already exist, you may find it beneficial to form one. Members should include an administrator; a teacher from each grade; a school counselor, school psychologist, or other school-based mental-health professional; a representative of the nonteaching staff; one or two parents; and other school personnel (for example, a nurse, school resource officer, Title IX representative), as appropriate.

### Materials Needed

☐ Copies of the *Cyberbullying* curriculum, one per person

☐ Name tags

☐ Marker

Duplicating this page is illegal. Do not copy this material without written permission from the publisher.

131

☐ Pens or pencils

☐ Masking tape

☐ Two pieces of poster board

☐ Your school's policy(ies) on bullying and cyberbullying, if available, as well as its policy on the acceptable use of technology

☐ Game pawns or small slips of paper

☐ CD-ROM materials:

- Peer Leader Packet 📄 I-10

- Glossary of Cyber Terms 📄 I-11

- Bullying Circle diagram 📄 S1-3

- Is It or Isn't It? Peer Leader Instructions, game board, and game cards 📄 S2-3, S2-4, S2-5

- Sessions 1–6 Journal Entries 📄 S1-1, S2-1, S3-1, S4-1, S5-1, S6-1

- Sessions 1–5 Real-Life Stories 📄 S1-2, S2-2, S3-2, S4-2, S5-2

- Homework Assignment 3 📄 S3-4 (SP)

- PSA Planning Sheet 📄 S4-3

- Do First poster and handout 📄 I-15, S5-3

- Social-Networking Site or App Planning Packet 📄 S6-3

☐ *Optional:* Smart Board or LCD projector for the additional background information on cyberbullying that is included as a Teacher Training Slideshow on the CD-ROM. 📄 I-14

☐ *Optional:* Refreshments (highly recommended)

## Preparation Needed

1. Select a training room in which participants will be comfortable sitting and interacting for 3 hours. Arrange the chairs in a circle or at small tables, so people

Duplicating this page is illegal. Do not copy this material without written permission from the publisher.

will be more open to discussing this sensitive topic with others. Also make sure the room temperature is comfortable.

2. *Optional:* Set up refreshments.

3. Read through this training outline and the curriculum, so you will be comfortable teaching others.

4. Write the Four Anti-Bullying Rules (session 1, page 51) on one sheet of poster board.

5. Create two columns on the second sheet of poster board and write these titles at the top of the columns:

   Traditional bullying is...          Cyberbullying is...

6. Photocopy the Is It or Isn't It? game board, instructions, and game cards to provide one game per group.

7. Highlight statistics from surveys of your own students (for example, from the *Olweus Bullying Questionnaire*) regarding bullying and cyberbullying. If these statistics are not available, research local or state statistics on bullying and/or cyberbullying, or use the statistics shown in the Teacher Training Slideshow on the CD-ROM. If using the Teacher Training Slideshow, you may want to print out a copy of the Training Handout for each participant and a copy of the Training Script for yourself.

   I-14

   *Optional:* Co-facilitate this training with someone who has a strong background in knowing these statistics.

8. Photocopy all other CD-ROM content to provide one set per person.

Duplicating this page is illegal. Do not copy this material without written permission from the publisher.

## Teacher Training Outline

**Introduction** (30 minutes)

1. Welcome participants and give each person a name tag if they may not all know each other.

2. Introduce yourself and your cotrainer(s) and briefly state why you have chosen to train others in the use of *Cyberbullying: A Prevention Curriculum for Grades 6–12.*

3. Have people introduce themselves and share briefly why they are interested in learning and teaching this cyberbullying curriculum.

4. Briefly describe the main content of the cyberbullying curriculum by paraphrasing the wording in the "Introduction to the Curriculum," pages 1–10.

5. Briefly describe the main components of the curriculum, including the eight sessions, which include the journal entries and real-life stories, the Is It or Isn't It? game, the public service announcements, the website/app project, and the parent-student homework assignments. Hand out copies of the *Cyberbullying* curriculum.

6. Highlight and discuss the introductory pages that describe what teachers should be aware of and other guidelines as they teach the curriculum (pages 7–10).

 I-14
7. *Optional:* Highlight statistics about the use of digital technology by children and youth (slides 2–4 of the Training Slideshow).

Duplicating this page is illegal. Do not copy this material without written permission from the publisher.

I-10

8. Discuss the importance of peer leaders when using this curriculum. Explain how they are chosen and what their roles will be. (If you are not giving copies of the curriculum to participants, make copies of the Peer Leader Packet, which is the I-10 file on the CD-ROM.)

### Defining Bullying (10 minutes)

1. As a group, discuss or review the definition of *bullying* (see page 45 or 49 in session 1 and slide 5 of the Training Slideshow).

S1-4

2. Display and discuss the Four Anti-Bullying Rules, from the *Olweus Bullying Prevention Program.* If your school is not already following these rules, discuss how they can be implemented in middle and high school classrooms.

S1-3

3. Distribute and discuss the Bullying Circle diagram and the roles that people play in bullying situations.

4. Briefly share school-level, local, or national statistics on bullying. Try to personalize this information as much as possible, so participants more clearly see the importance of addressing this issue with their students.

### Defining Cyberbullying (20 minutes)

1. Divide participants into groups of three or four people. Have them brainstorm a list of ways that people can cyberbully.

2. Have each group briefly share a few ideas from its list. Add to the discussion, as necessary, using slides 9–15.

3. Discuss the differences and similarities between traditional forms of bullying and cyberbullying. Write these ideas on a sheet of poster board that has been prepared following the format in session 2, part 1, starting at step 5 on page 60. (See also slides 6–8.)

Duplicating this page is illegal. Do not copy this material without written permission from the publisher.

4. Keep participants in their groups. Hand out the Is It or Isn't It? instructions, game board, game cards, and the pawns or slips of paper. If you're using slips of paper, have participants write their names on them and use these in place of game pawns. Allow groups to play the game to give them a better understanding of what cyberbullying is and how students will be using this game.

S2-3
S2-4
S2-5

5. Hand out the Glossary of Cyber Terms and briefly go through the terms and their definitions.

I-11

6. Briefly share school-level, local, or national statistics on cyberbullying (slides 16–17).

I-14

## The Effects of Cyberbullying (30 minutes)

1. Share the warning signs or "red flags" that someone may be cyberbullying others or being cyberbullied (see "Introduction to Cyberbullying," pages 11–18). Stress the importance of teachers' being aware of these warning signs, being proactive in talking with these students to determine what is wrong, and taking action when necessary.

I-14

2. *Optional:* Review some of the data from the CD-ROM's Teacher Training file on possible effects of cyberbullying on students (slides 22–27).

3. Hand out the Journal Entries and Real-Life Stories. Briefly describe how these are used in each session.

4. Have participants turn to the Session 3 Journal Entries and Session 3 Real-Life Story. Split the participants into five groups of at least two people each, depending on group size. Assign each group a journal entry or the real-life story. They are to read their assigned selection and answer the discussion questions. (If you do not have enough participants to form five groups, create smaller groups or assign more than one selection to one or more groups.) Give the groups 5 minutes to do this. (Allow more time if there are groups assigned to more than one selection.)

S3-1
S3-2

Duplicating this page is illegal. Do not copy this material without written permission from the publisher.

137

5. Invite each group to read its journal entry or story aloud and answer the questions. (Be sure to use the following order when having groups read aloud the entries: Allie, J.T., Serena, Aaron.) After each group finishes, open the floor for discussion. The point of going through this process is to give participants a better understanding of how cyberbullying can affect tweens and teens and how these activities will be used in classes.

6. Briefly discuss what students will do for the positive digital support activity and discuss the value of encouraging positive use of technology (see pages 78–79).

7. Hand out Homework Assignment 3 so participants have the ABCs of Cyberbullying Prevention. Discuss any points that may be unclear.

S3-4

### Break (10 minutes)

1. *Optional:* Provide refreshments.

### Why People Cyberbully (10 minutes)

1. Discuss why people cyberbully others (session 4, part 1, starting with step 6, page 86 or step 5 on page 87).

2. If available, read and discuss your school's policy on cyberbullying. If your school has a policy on bullying that does not specifically mention cyberbullying, discuss how the policy may relate to cyberbullying on (or off) campus. (See the CD-ROM for more information about development of policies on cyberbullying.) If your school does not have a cyberbullying policy, it may have a policy regarding acceptable use of technology that mentions cyberbullying and or other inappropriate uses of campus technology.

I-2

I-3

I-7

### Public Service Announcements (PSAs) (20 minutes)

1. Explain the PSA activity from session 4, part 2, to the group (see pages 90–92).

Duplicating this page is illegal. Do not copy this material without written permission from the publisher.

2. Split the participants into groups of three or four people. Hand out a PSA Planning Sheet to each group member. Give groups 10 minutes to brainstorm what they would do for a PSA to stop cyberbullying. Encourage them to write down their ideas.

3. Convene the entire group and invite each small group to share what its PSA would be.

## What Can We Do to Stop and Prevent Cyberbullying? (20 minutes)

1. Distribute the Do First poster and handout.

   I-15
   S5-3

2. Discuss the handout and how teachers and other school staff can help students feel more comfortable reporting incidents of cyberbullying.

3. Take time to discuss your school's reporting policy of cyberbullying incidents for teachers and other school staff. Be sure to talk about situations when the police should be involved, for example, if the cyberbullying is racially motivated, includes threats to harm, or is defamatory in nature.

## Creating a Positive Social-Networking Site or App (10 minutes)

1. Take some time to explain this activity from sessions 6–8.

   Introduce the premise for the activity:

   TechyTeen Company is interested in investing 25 million dollars in a new social-networking site or app that encourages safe and positive interactions among tweens and teens.

   Explain the criteria that students will be using to create their plans for their sites or apps:

   • how strongly the sites or apps appeal to tweens and teens

   • how safe they are

   • how well they promote positive interactions among tweens, teens, and their world

   Hand out the Social-Networking Site or App Planning Packet to give participants an idea of how detailed the project should be.

   S6-3

Duplicating this page is illegal. Do not copy this material without written permission from the publisher.

**Concluding Activities** (20 minutes)

1. If you have a group of school educators, be sure to share with them the Curriculum Scope and Sequence, page 19, and the Related National Academic Standards, pages 21–24. Using *Cyberbullying* can also help you meet several Common Core Standards; see www.violencepreventionworks .org for more information.

2. Take time to answer any questions participants may have. Also spend time discussing any special adaptations that may be needed for their specific situations.

3. Finish by having participants discuss and write down several goals for using *Cyberbullying: A Prevention Curriculum for Grades 6–12*. On a piece of paper, have participants write their basic plan, for example, by answering these questions:

   • When will implementation begin?

   • How often will the curriculum be taught?

   • During what class(es)?

   • How will efforts be evaluated?

   It is important that participants have concrete plans for implementation when they leave your training.

4. Thank everyone for attending. Consider giving participants certificates for their participation in the workshop, or check into whether participants can receive credit toward staff development or professional learning units.

Duplicating this page is illegal. Do not copy this material without written permission from the publisher.

## Additional Resources

### Recommended Readings

Goodstein, Anastasia. 2007. *Totally Wired: What Teens and Tweens Are Really Doing Online.* New York: St. Martin's Griffin.

Kowalski, Robin M., Susan P. Limber, and Patricia W. Agatston. 2012. *Cyberbullying: Bullying in the Digital Age.* 2nd ed. Malden, MA: Wiley-Blackwell.

Patchin, Justin W., ed., and Sameer Hinduja, ed. 2012. *Cyberbullying Prevention and Response: Expert Perspectives.* New York: Routledge.

Willard, Nancy E. 2007. *Cyberbullying and Cyberthreats: Responding to the Challenge of Online Social Aggression, Threats, and Distress.* Champaign, IL: Research Press.

Willard, Nancy E. 2007. *Cyber-Safe Kids, Cyber-Savvy Teens: Helping Young People Learn to Use the Internet Safely and Responsibly.* New York: Jossey-Bass.

### Online Resources

**www.violencepreventionworks.org** This website contains information about bullying and cyberbullying.

**www.cyberbullyhelp.com** This website includes general information about cyberbullying and information specifically targeted to parents and students. Viewers of the site can also read excerpts from the book *Cyberbullying: Bullying in the Digital Age.*

Duplicating this page is illegal. Do not copy this material without written permission from the publisher.

141

**www.stopbullyingnow.gov** This interactive website sponsored by the Federal Partners in Bullying Prevention provides extensive information about bullying, with specific information about cyberbullying.

**www.commonsensemedia.org** This nonprofit organization advocates on child and family issues, and studies the effects that media and technology have on young users. The website also addresses cyberbullying and digital literacy and citizenship.

**www.connectsafely.com** This Internet safety site designed for parents, teens, and experts provides information to facilitate "smart socializing" online and through mobile phones. The site has helpful tips and information regarding the newest forms of technology.

**www.ikeepsafe.org** The Internet Keep Safe Coalition was created in 2005 to track trends and issues with digital products and their effects on children. Teachers can access K–12 digital citizenship materials to implement in their schools. Additionally, this nonprofit offers an app to assess your knowledge of digital issues.

**www.wiredsafety.org** An interactive website created by Internet privacy and security lawyer Parry Aftab, this site provides information about cyberbullying and related online abuses.

**www.netsmartz.org** Sponsored by the National Center for Missing and Exploited Children, NetSmartz.org is devoted to providing information about Internet safety to children, parents, educators, and law-enforcement officials.

**www.cdc.gov/violenceprevention/youthviolence/electronicaggression /index.html** This site, maintained by the Centers for Disease Control and Prevention, provides an overview of cyberbullying, as well as links to several articles published by leading researchers in the field of cyberbullying in a special issue of the *Journal of Adolescent Health*.

**www.ryanpatrickhalligan.org** When he was thirteen, Ryan Patrick Halligan died by suicide as a result of being cyberbullied. His parents have created this website focusing on Internet safety, bullying, cyberbullying, and suicide.

Duplicating this page is illegal. Do not copy this material without written permission from the publisher.

## Video and Digital Resources

***Cyberbully*** This 2011 made-for-TV movie was created by ABC Family and *Seventeen* magazine. The film tells the story of a teenage girl who is bullied online. She eventually finds a support group and learns to stand up for herself and, as a result, inspires others to stand up as well.

***Adina's Deck*** This DVD program is designed to disseminate information about cyberbullying to nine- to fifteen-year-olds. It has a companion website, www.adinasdeck.com, and a teacher's guide.

***Submit the Documentary*** This educational film tells stories of families affected by cyberbullying. It has a companion website at www.submitthedocumentary.com.

Duplicating this page is illegal. Do not copy this material without written permission from the publisher.

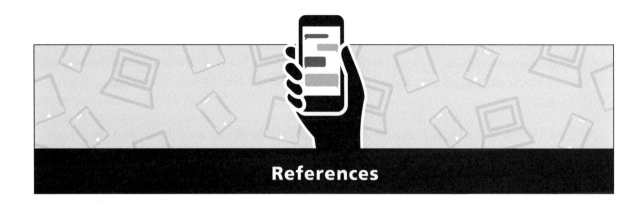

# References

Arseneault, Louise, Elizabeth Walsh, Kali Trzesniewski, Rhiannon Newcombe, Ashalom Caspi, and Terrie E. Moffitt. 2006. "Bullying Victimization Uniquely Contributes to Adjustment Problems in Young Children: A Nationally Representative Cohort Study." *Pediatrics* 118 (1): 130–38.

Eisenberg, Marla E., Dianne Neumark-Sztainer, and Cheryl Perry. 2003. "Peer Harassment, School Connectedness, and Academic Achievement." *Journal of School Health* 73 (8): 311–16.

Espelage, Dorothy L., and Melissa K. Holt. 2013. "Suicidal Ideation and School Bullying Experiences after Controlling for Depression and Delinquency." *Journal of Adolescent Health* 53 (1): S27–S31.

Fekkes, Minne, Frans I. M. Pijpers, and S. Pauline Verloove-VanHorick. 2004. "Bullying Behavior and Associations with Psychosomatic Complaints and Depression in Victims." *Journal of Pediatrics* 144 (1): 17–22.

Klomek, Anat B., Frank Marrocco, Marjorie Kleinman, Irvin S. Schonfeld, and Madelyn S. Gould. 2008. "Peer Victimization, Depression, and Suicidality in Adolescents." *Suicide and Life-Threatening Behavior* 38 (2): 166–80.

Kowalski, Robin M., Gary W. Giumetti, Amber N. Schroeder, and Micah Lattanner. 2014. "Bullying in the Digital Age: A Critical Review and Meta-analysis of Cyberbullying Research among Youth." *Psychological Bulletin* 140 (4): 1073–1137. http://dx.doi.org/10.1037/a0035618.

Kowalski, Robin M., and Susan P. Limber. 2007. "Electronic Bullying among Middle School Students." *Journal of Adolescent Health* 41 (6): S22–S30.

Kowalski, Robin M., and Susan P. Limber. 2013. "Psychological, Physical, and Academic Correlates of Cyberbullying and Traditional Bullying." *Journal of Adolescent Health* 53 (1): S13–S20.

Kowalski, Robin M., Susan P. Limber, and Patricia W. Agatston. 2012. *Cyberbullying: Bullying in the Digital Age*. 2nd ed. Malden, MA: Wiley-Blackwell.

Duplicating this page is illegal. Do not copy this material without written permission from the publisher.

Nakamoto, Jonathan, and David Schwartz. 2010. "Is Peer Victimization Associated with Academic Achievement? A Meta-analytic Review." *Social Development* 19 (2): 221–42.

Olweus, Dan. 1993. *Bullying at School: What We Know and What We Can Do.* Malden, MA: Blackwell Publishing.

Olweus, Dan, Susan P. Limber, Vicki Crocker Flerx, Nancy Mullin, Jane Riese, and Marlene Snyder. 2007. *Olweus Bullying Prevention Program: Teacher Guide.* Center City, MN: Hazelden Publishing.

Prancjić, Nurka, and Amila Bajraktarević. 2010. "Depression and Suicide Ideation among Secondary School Adolescents Involved in School Bullying." *Primary Health Care Research and Development* 11 (4): 349–62.

Rigby, Ken, and Phillip T. Slee. 1993. "Dimensions of Interpersonal Relations among Australian School Children and Their Implications for Psychological Well-Being." *Journal of Social Psychology* 133 (1): 33–42.

Robers, Simone, Jana Kemp, Jennifer Truman, and Thomas D. Snyder. 2013. *Indicators of School Crime and Safety: 2012* (NCES 2013-036/NCJ 241446). Washington, DC: National Center for Education Statistics, U.S. Department of Education, and Bureau of Justice Statistics, Office of Justice Programs, U.S. Department of Justice.

Snyder, Marlene, Jane Riese, Susan P. Limber, Dan Olweus, and Stein Gorseth. 2014. *Olweus Bullying Prevention Program: Community Youth Organization Guide.* Center City, MN: Hazelden Publishing.

Wang, Jing, Tonja R. Nansel, and Ronald J. Iannotti. 2011. "Cyber Bullying and Traditional Bullying: Differential Association with Depression." *Journal of Adolescent Health* 48 (4): 415–17.

Willard, Nancy E. 2007. "Educator's Guide to Cyberbullying and Cyberthreats." Center for Safe and Responsible Internet Use. Retrieved November 15, 2007, from www.cyberbully.org.

Duplicating this page is illegal. Do not copy this material without written permission from the publisher.

## About the Authors

### Susan P. Limber, Ph.D.

Dr. Susan P. Limber is the Dan Olweus professor within the Institute on Family and Neighborhood Life at Clemson University. She is a developmental psychologist who received her master's and doctoral degrees in psychology at the University of Nebraska–Lincoln. She also holds a master's of legal studies from Nebraska.

Dr. Limber's research and writing have focused on legal and psychological issues related to youth violence, particularly bullying among children, child protection, and children's rights. She directed the first wide-scale implementation and evaluation of the *Olweus Bullying Prevention Program* in the United States and coauthored the *Blueprint for the Bullying Prevention Program*, as well as many other articles on the topic of bullying. In recent years, she has overseen the dissemination of the *Olweus Bullying Prevention Program* in the United States. She has provided consultation on bullying research to the Health Resources and Services Administration.

Dr. Limber has been recognized with several awards for her work, including the American Psychological Association's (APA) Early Career Award for Psychology in the Public Interest (2004), the Distinguished Career Award for Outstanding Contributions to Public Service Psychology (2011 by the Division of Psychologists in Public Service, APA), and the Nicholas Hobbs Award (2012, Society for Child and Family Policy and Practice, APA).

Duplicating this page is illegal. Do not copy this material without written permission from the publisher.

## Robin M. Kowalski, Ph.D.

Dr. Robin M. Kowalski is a professor of psychology at Clemson University. She obtained her doctoral degree in social psychology from the University of North Carolina at Greensboro. Her research interests focus primarily on aversive interpersonal behaviors, most notably complaining, teasing, and bullying, with a particular focus on cyberbullying. She is the author or coauthor of several books, including *Complaining, Teasing, and Other Annoying Behaviors; Social Anxiety; Aversive Interpersonal Behaviors; Behaving Badly; The Social Psychology of Emotional and Behavioral Problems;* and *Cyberbullying: Bullying in the Digital Age.* Her research on complaining brought her international attention, including an appearance on NBC's *Today Show.*

Dr. Kowalski has received several awards, including Clemson University's Award of Distinction, Clemson University's College of Business and Behavioral Science Award for Excellence in Undergraduate Teaching, the Phil Prince Award for Excellence and Innovation in Teaching, and the Clemson Board of Trustees Award for Faculty Excellence. She was also a 2013 and 2014 finalist for the South Carolina Governor's Professor of the Year Award.

## Patricia W. Agatston, Ph.D.

Patricia W. Agatston, Ph.D., is coauthor of the book *Cyberbullying: Bullying in the Digital Age* with Robin Kowalski, Ph.D., and Susan Limber, Ph.D., and has coauthored a chapter for the book *Cyberbullying Prevention and Response: Expert Perspectives.* Dr. Agatston is a certified trainer and technical assistance consultant for the *Olweus Bullying Prevention Program.* She has been quoted in articles on cyberbullying in the *Washington Post*, CNET news, *Time*, and the *Christian Science Monitor.* She has appeared on CNN, as well as other local and national radio and television programs, to discuss cyberbullying and other youth online risky behavior. She was a participant in the Centers for Disease Control and Prevention's (CDC) Expert Panel on Electronic Media and Youth Violence and in the CDC's Expert Panel on Youth Involvement in Bullying and Suicide-Related Behaviors. She has presented nationally and internationally on bullying, cyberbullying, and digital citizenship.

Dr. Agatston is a licensed professional counselor and prevention specialist with the Cobb County School District's Prevention/Intervention Center in Marietta, Georgia. She serves on the board of directors for the International Bullying Prevention Association and ConnectSafely.

Duplicating this page is illegal. Do not copy this material without written permission from the publisher.

**Hazelden,** a national nonprofit organization founded in 1949, helps people reclaim their lives from the disease of addiction. Built on decades of knowledge and experience, Hazelden offers a comprehensive approach to addiction that addresses the full range of patient, family, and professional needs, including treatment and continuing care for youth and adults, research, higher learning, public education and advocacy, and publishing.

A life of recovery is lived "one day at a time." Hazelden publications, both educational and inspirational, support and strengthen lifelong recovery. In 1954, Hazelden published *Twenty-Four Hours a Day*, the first daily meditation book for recovering alcoholics, and Hazelden continues to publish works to inspire and guide individuals in treatment and recovery, and their loved ones. Professionals who work to prevent and treat addiction also turn to Hazelden for evidence-based curricula, informational materials, and videos for use in schools, treatment programs, and correctional programs.

Through published works, Hazelden extends the reach of hope, encouragement, help, and support to individuals, families, and communities affected by addiction and related issues.

For questions about Hazelden publications, please call **800-328-9000** or visit us online at **hazelden.org/bookstore**.